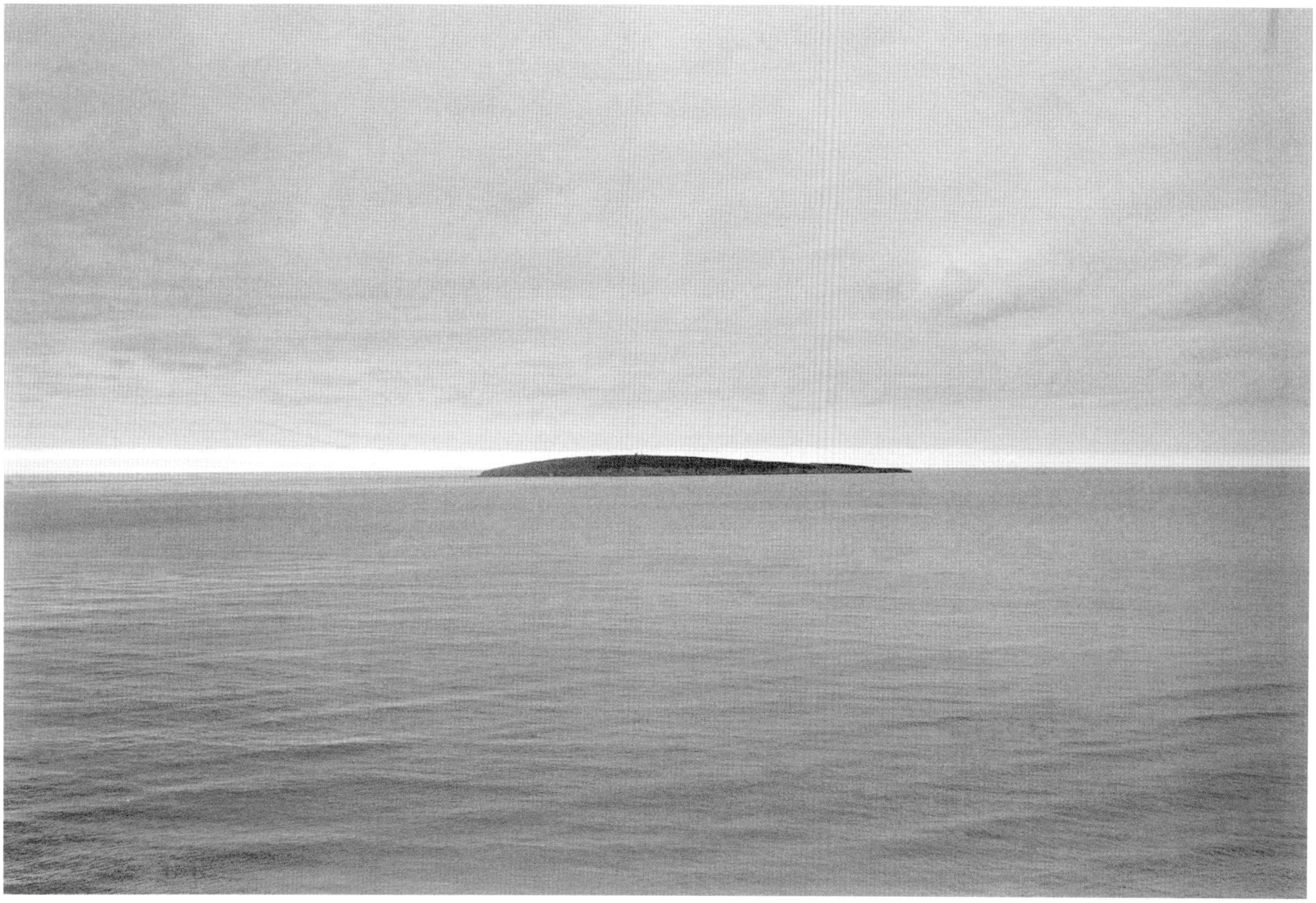

Summers with Extraordinary People

MAGNETIC NORTH

ROBERTA NEIMAN

Joost Elffers Books

Joost Elffers Books, New York, NY
Published and printed: 2018, USA
Printed by Earth Enterprise
Text set in Hoefler and Akzidenz-Grotesk

Front cover photo:
Richard Serra climbing up A-Frame

Opening and closing page photo:
Margaree Island, Cape Breton

Page 8: *Roberta and Joey down along the cove*
photo attributed to Rudy Wurlitzer

Page 37: *Joan, Roberta and JoAnne*
photo attributed to Rudy Wurlitzer

Page 75: *June and Roberta*
photo attributed to Robert Frank

Page 80: *Costume drama #2: Roberta and Rudy*
photo attributed to Richard Serra

Page 104: *Roberta Neiman*
photo attributed to Jon Wolf

SPECIAL THANKS TO
Gabriela Carrasco Escobar, Massimo Audiello, Rodrigo Carus, Antonio Turok, Greg Neiman, Max Blagg, Janice Huminska

And thank you to Ronald Chapman
for use of MAGNETIC NORTH™

Text: Roberta Neiman
Text Edit: Max Blagg
Book Design: Patricia Childers

ISBN: 9780971897526

For Toby Rafelson

Photography is tied to specifying, and in Roberta Neiman's book the images pay attention to the definition of a time and a place in Cape Breton, Nova Scotia, over four decades ago, where a group of writers, actors, filmmakers, performers, musicians and artists of every description came together, exchanged thoughts and explored ideas, separately and in collaboration. Remarkably, for the most part, everybody got along. This was a random chance, being in the right place at the right time, a young group of fearless people sharing the wonder and beauty of a desolate island in the far north. There existed an unspoken recognition that having landed together we could live and learn from each other.

Richard Serra

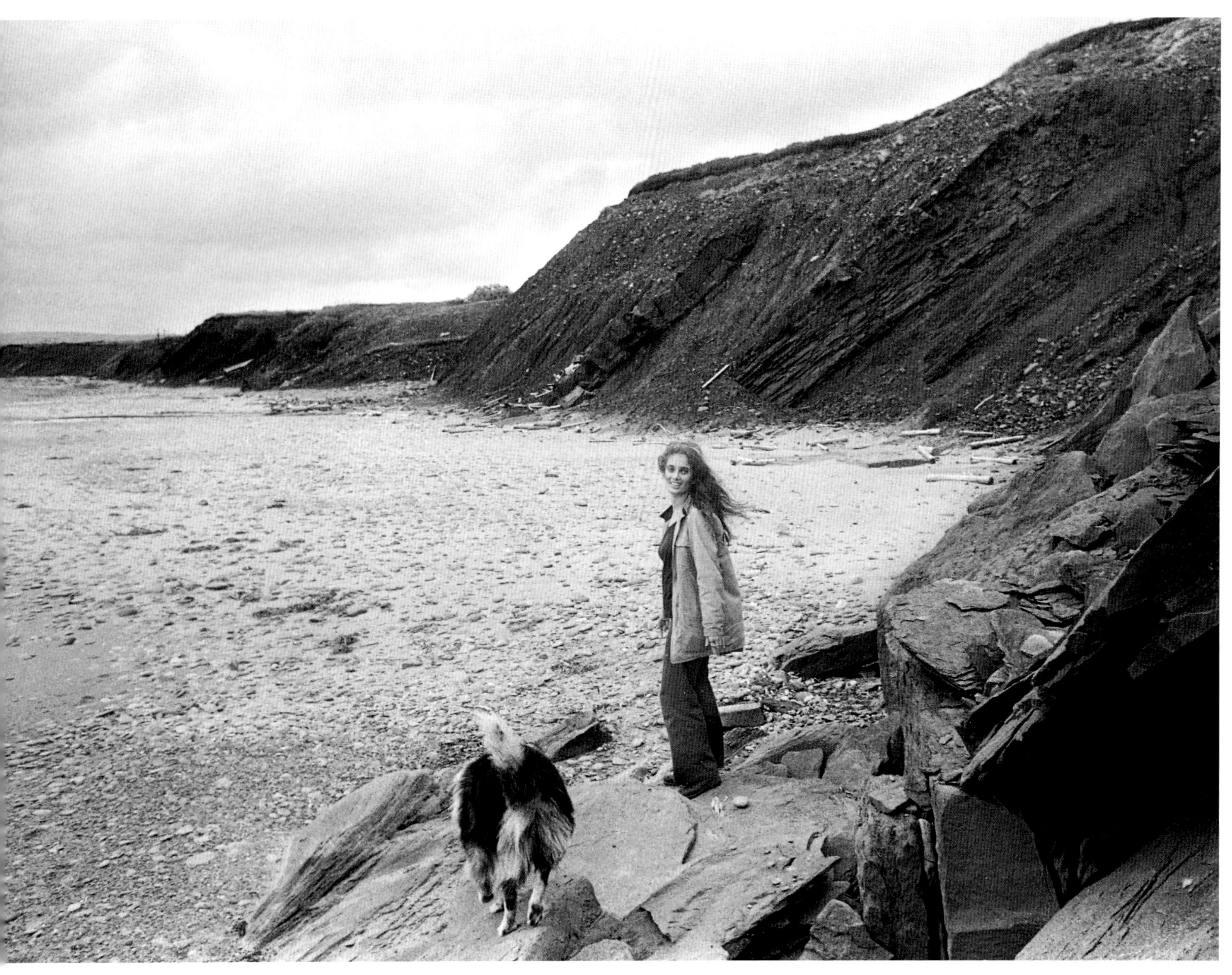

I grew up in the 1950's in Los Angeles, wearing white gloves and dressed in pastel colors.

My father was in a business no-one talked about, and my mother spent a lot of time at the mirror, worrying about her looks, wondering who she was. I was raised to drive a car, be pretty, go to college and secure a husband who was either a doctor or a lawyer. I followed this path and married a law student with a great sense of humor and a terrible temper. One day, as I cautiously ironed his shirts while watching I Love Lucy on our tiny black and white TV set, I realized this was not the life I wanted to lead.

Soon after this revelation, I abandoned my domestic duties and fled to the art department at UCLA, where my art instructor and I fell madly in love. He helped me to get a job at the Ferus Gallery, one of the most important art galleries in L.A. at the time. It was run by two very cool guys, Walter Hopps and Irving Blum, who initiated me into a world that was wildly eccentric and utterly intriguing. An important day in my new life was when the artist Billy Al Bengston stormed into the gallery and proceeded to verbally abuse Irving Blum with the most astounding barrage of profanity I'd ever heard. I knew I was in the right place.

I first met Rudy Wurlitzer toward the end of 1969, when we were introduced in a dark Hollywood movie theater by a mutual friend. He already had a reputation as a remarkable writer and he was living at the old Tropicana Motel, working on a film script. Tall and sandy-haired, his blue-eyed gaze was inescapably seductive, and I was captivated. Some weeks later, Rudy invited me to spend the following summer with him on Cape Breton Island, where he had just bought property with his college friend Philip Glass, a place to work undisturbed by the demands of city life.

Since I had recently been considering leaving Los Angeles, the timing of Rudy's invitation was perfect, and we went back together to New York City, and spent the winter there. In the following months, I read his novel *Nog*, more than once. The book was unlike any book I'd previously encountered. It was hard to fathom. Time and space were chopped and rechanneled, reality drifted loose from its moorings. Whatever was happening, it was a wild poetic ride, intense, delirious, utterly strange.

Spring came, and it was finally warm enough to make the long trek up to Canada. Rudy and I and my twelve year old son, Greg, set out for Cape Breton in the early summer of 1970, driving an old station wagon with a canoe strapped to the roof. We drove north for three days and finally reached Nova Scotia and then Cape Breton Island. On a late afternoon in June, we passed through Inverness, the last town before reaching Rudy and Philip's property. Immediately upon arriving at the camp, we got out of the station wagon and followed Rudy to the edge of the cliff, which dropped precipitously to a rocky beach far below. We stood facing west, towards the sun setting on the vast, open expanse of the St. Lawrence Bay and the ocean beyond. The intense silvery North Atlantic light, the rugged, windblown landscape, and the endless space surrounding us was almost overwhelming.

The site had been an old hunting camp, with a large, gray-shingled lodge visible on the land behind us—"The Big House," as it was called, and eleven rustic A-frame cabins in the surrounding woods. From somewhere in the distance I heard the sounds of shouting children and barking dogs mixing in the air with a strange, mercurial music. I was entering into an unknown world, far from my experience. A new world, peopled by an extraordinary cast of characters; a harmonic convergence of artists, writers, musicians and dancers, most of whom I photographed as they worked and played here in Cape Breton's brief, idyllic summers. There was a true sense of camaraderie and shared inspiration. And mutual admiration for the intense creativity in which we were immersed. The list is long and distinguished, and includes Philip Glass, Rudy Wurlitzer, JoAnne Akalaitis, Richard Serra, Joan Jonas, Robert Frank, June Leaf, Steve Katz, Helen Tworkov, James Strahs, and other visitors, including Pat Steir, Toby Rafelson, Keith Sonnier, Jackie Windsor, Tony Shafrazi. Many of them still return to Cape Breton, a magical place that continues to have a deep and lasting effect.

Rudy and Philip had purchased the lodge from a local named John-Dan MacPherson, whose family descended from a long line of fishermen. MacPhersons had owned all the land around them for generations, but they had big families and money was always short, so they decided to sell—originally to an American business man with big ideas for what he would do with it. Nothing came of those plans. When Philip and Rudy came along, they persuaded the new owner to sell it to them.

After purchasing the land, they realized, with great satisfaction, that John-Dan MacPherson was part of the deal. He knew everything about the place, and still fished the waters and put out his lobster pots most every day. John-Dan and his family lived on a piece of land next to us. They and the rest of the locals were tolerant of us, even if they thought we were nuts. There were seventeen MacPherson children, which, added to our seven, meant there were a lot of kids around. Our own bunch were resourceful, always creating their own amusements.

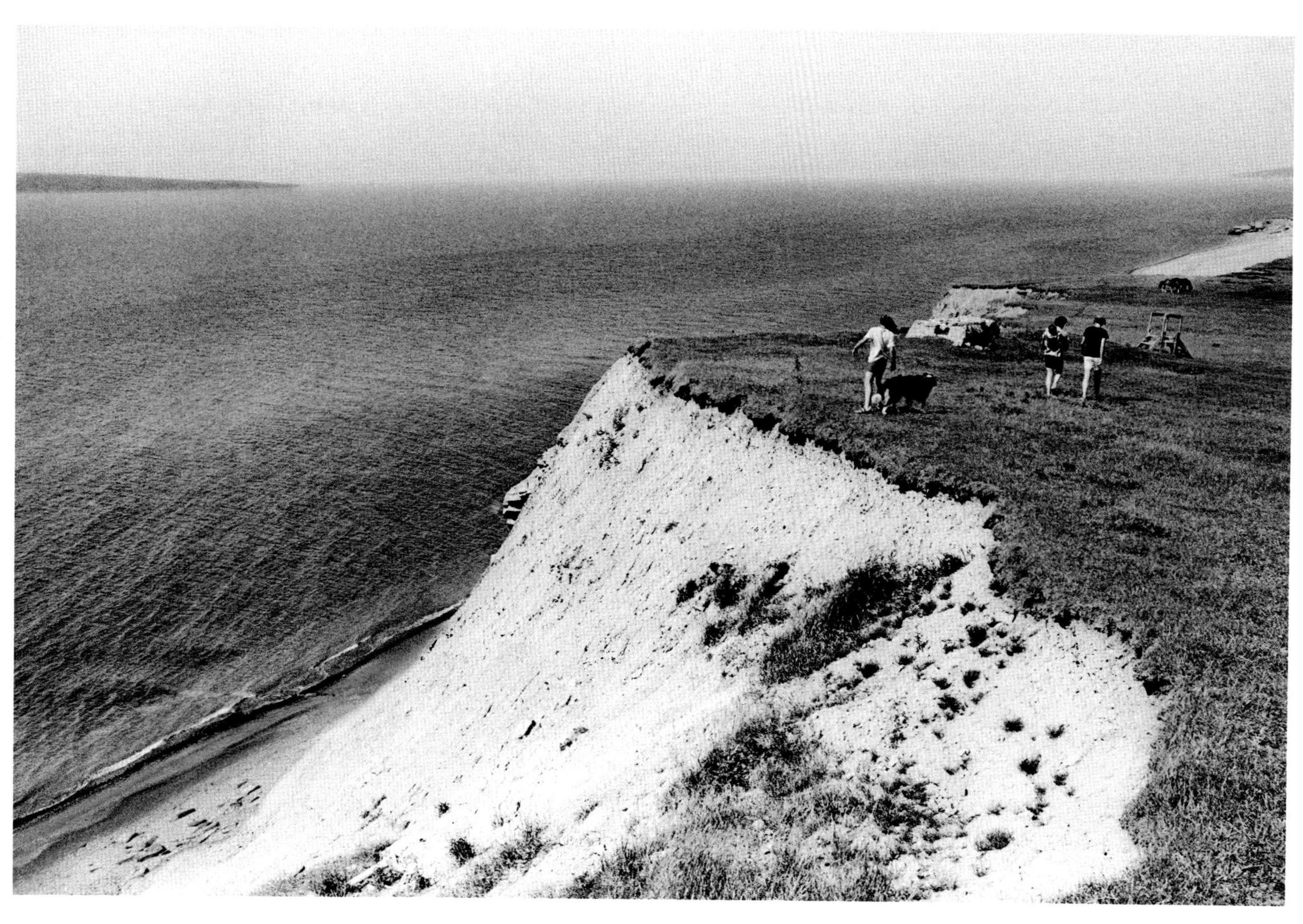

View from the clifftop

The MacPherson kids would wander in and out of the houses, looking wide-eyed and sideways at this crazy band of gypsies who had set down in their midst.

In early June of 1970, Philip and his then-wife, theater director JoAnne Akalaitis, had arrived at the property with their daughter, Juliet, ahead of everyone else, to get settled and start a garden. Being a family, they took over The Big House, and by the time we arrived they had things fairly well set up, with JoAnne as head cook and camp boss. The rest of us worked and slept in the small A-frames (without water or power) scattered around the property. During the day, we worked on our various projects and fended for ourselves in the large communal kitchen. In the afternoons we congregated at the beach for swimming and gossip and long walks. Our neighbors went there, too. Talk was of the weather, fishing, what's for dinner. In the evening, we usually gathered for meals at the ample dining table and shared the large common room for conversation, games, and general entertainment. There was endless creativity, chaos, and a strong sense of individuality in our community.

That first summer, Philip brought his original ensemble up to Cape Breton—Kurt Munkacsi, Michael Riesman and Philip on keyboards, Dickie Landry, Jon Gibson and Richard Peck playing winds—to work on Music With Changing Parts. The group worked in the communal area of The Big House during the day. Philip was relaxed in this environment, which seemed to give him and his musicians more creative freedom. JoAnne had also invited the entire company of a new theater group that she was directing, named Mabou Mines after a nearby town, to come up for the summer and develop new work. Philip helped build a rehearsal studio, and he was especially proud of the sonic qualities of the stage he had constructed.

Later that summer, at the invitation of Philip and Rudy, the sculptor Richard Serra and performance artist Joan Jonas arrived together for a visit. Also taken by the light and landscape of Cape Breton, they bought an old farmhouse with a large barn for Richard's studio. (The year following, Joan sold her share to Richard and bought herself a house on the cliffs nearby). Joan Jonas had a powerful affinity for ghost stories and ghosts, and Cape Breton was filled with both, which aligned perfectly with her shamanic tendencies. On her birthday, she created a performance on the beach and invited everyone to attend. She gave each person some small token, a rock, a shell that she had gathered on her long beach walks. The object was now imbued with Joan's own magical sensibility. During those precious summers, there were many events like this, ephemeral, spontaneous performances witnessed by a fortunate few. They always had a marvelous resonance. They found a place in your memory.

Robert Frank and June Leaf had also recently landed in Cape Breton. Seeking a change of pace from the intensity of New York, Robert asked June to find them an isolated spot somewhere far from the city. In the midst of a freezing winter, his resourceful partner found an old abandoned farmhouse at the end of a dirt road, overlooking the sea, in the small fishing village of Mabou Mines. Despite the primitive conditions and unforgiving climate, they commenced

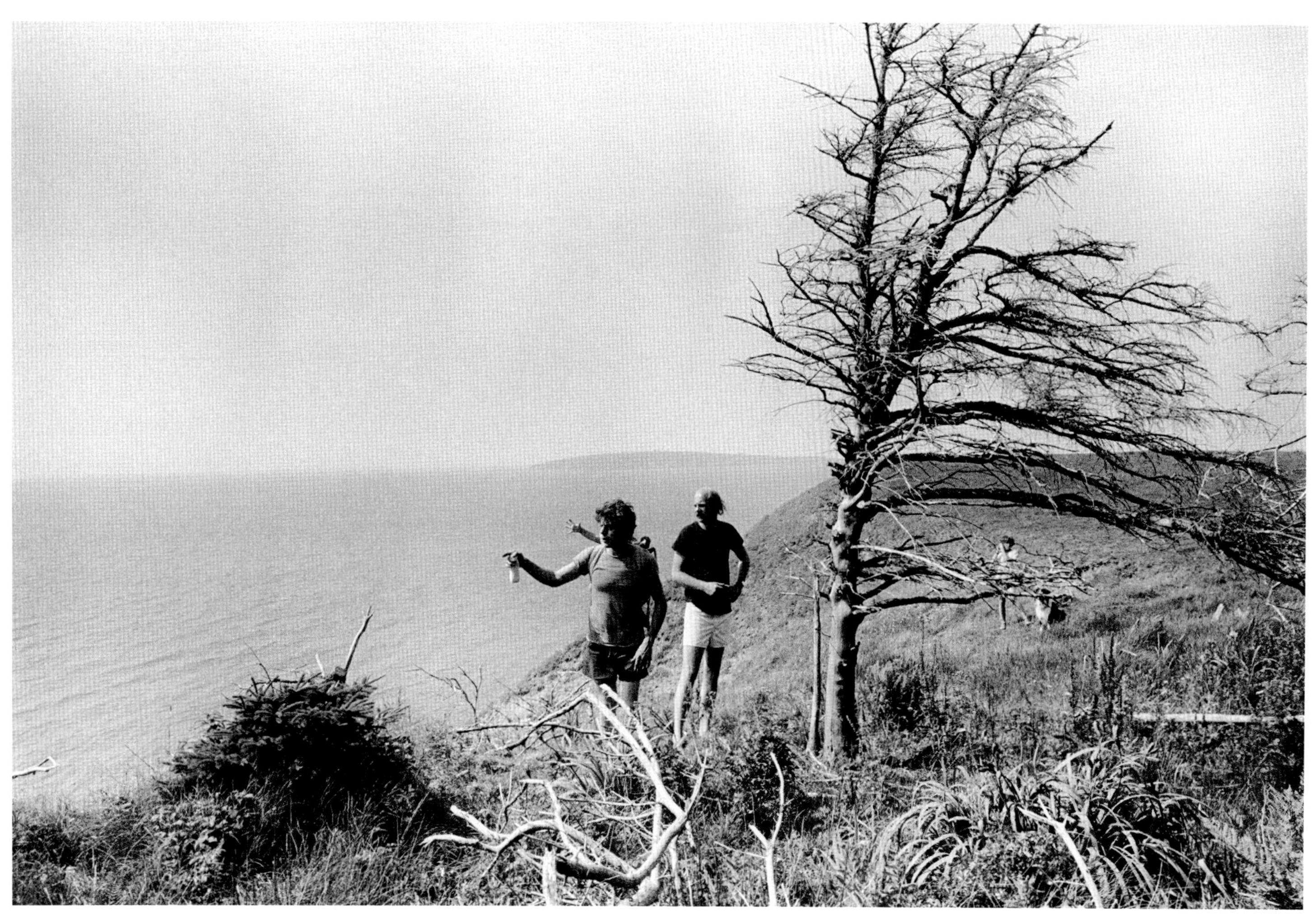

Phillip and Rudy

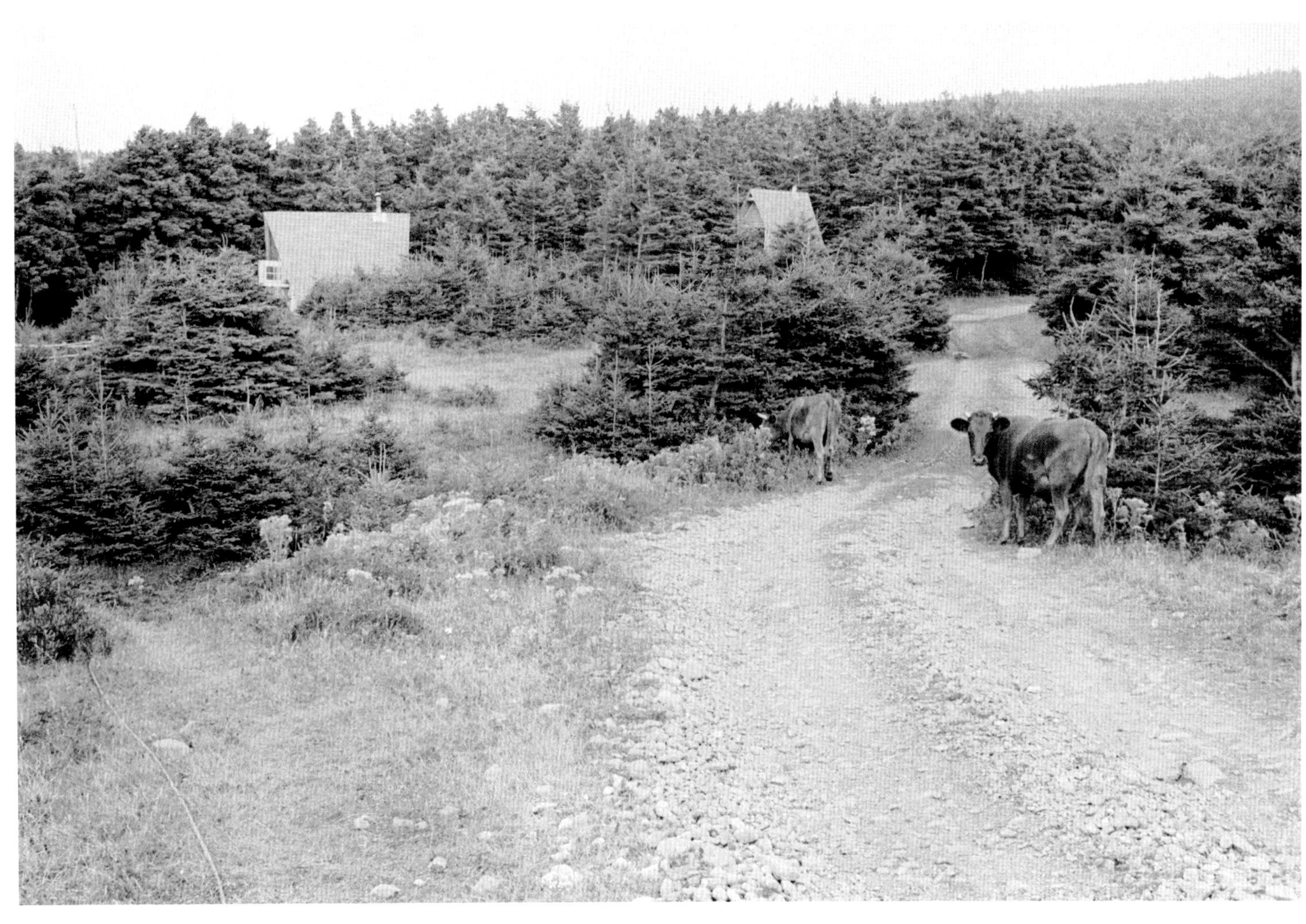

A-frames in the woods, cows in the road

to live there year-round for the next several years. When we arrived, they generously shared all kinds of useful information that helped us begin to fathom the idiosyncratic nature of Cape Breton.

Always looking for new adventures, we sometimes rowed out to Margaree Island, known locally as Sea Wolf Island. It lay out in the bay, its long smooth outline visible to anyone who lived along the coast. An abandoned lighthouse on its bare hilltop was the subject of many myths and rumors. Rowing there took about an hour and our boat often encountered the whales that summered in the Bay, their smooth rounded contours strikingly similar to the island's own silhouette. Margaree seemed to float just above the waters, a constant and mysterious presence. Treeless and windswept, it still harbored several old, broken-down fishing shacks, most without roofs, others pierced with eerie beams of light revealing dark interiors, knee deep in smashed lobster traps, rotted nets and discarded buoys. I became quite obsessed with the island and tried to include it in as many of my pictures as I could.

The closest link we had to the outside world was a pay phone in Dunvegan, a town in Inverness closest to our settlement. Rudy and I often went there, and he would spend hours folded into the town's only public phone booth, engaged in endless conversations. He loved the phone, and he was in a major creative phase, working on novels as well as screenplays. I walked around the town talking to townspeople and taking photographs while he talked to Hollywood. He had just published the post-apocalyptic novel, *Flats* (1970), which was even more eccentric than *Nog*. He had also written a screenplay for director Monte Hellman's existential road movie, *Two Lane Blacktop (Esquire* Magazine published the script in its entirety), and was plotting *Quake* (1972), a dystopian nightmare that seems ominously prescient in our current political climate.

During our second summer, Rudy and I built a small comfortable cabin in the woods, overlooking the cliffs. Greg and I had lived in the ski town of Aspen, Colorado, when it was still very small, so we were not strangers to spartan living conditions. We scavenged what we could from two of the abandoned A-frames. Rudy, with a lot of help from our neighbor, John-Dan Macpherson, built the house. I built some of the interiors (the white gloves had long been discarded) and what I thought was a great kitchen with a large table. The place became a social center for the only serious competition between us all, some highly charged poker games.

In 1972 the writer Steve Katz had accepted an invitation to come to Cape Breton with his family. He and his wife Jingle (Pat Bell) and their boys Rafael, Avrum, and Nikolai, stayed in various A-frames on the property before buying land nearby. With the help of several friends and their three sons, Steve and Jingle built a crooked wooden tower, and soon after that, a slightly imperfect teepee. Jingle was well suited to the natural way of life there, tending to her rabbits and vegetable garden. And though she rarely came to The Big House, we were often invited for a meal over their campfire.

Roberta Neiman

In 1969, the idea of finding a place outside of the city began to occupy me. My partner in this search was my friend, Rudy Wurlitzer. I had known Rudy from my time at Juilliard. Rudy was one of the few writers I knew who had actually published a book. We both wanted to find somewhere to work and get away from New York. We knew that any part of the U.S. east coast was already too expensive. A friend, Peter Moore, mentioned Cape Breton, Nova Scotia, which sounded perfect.

Philip Glass

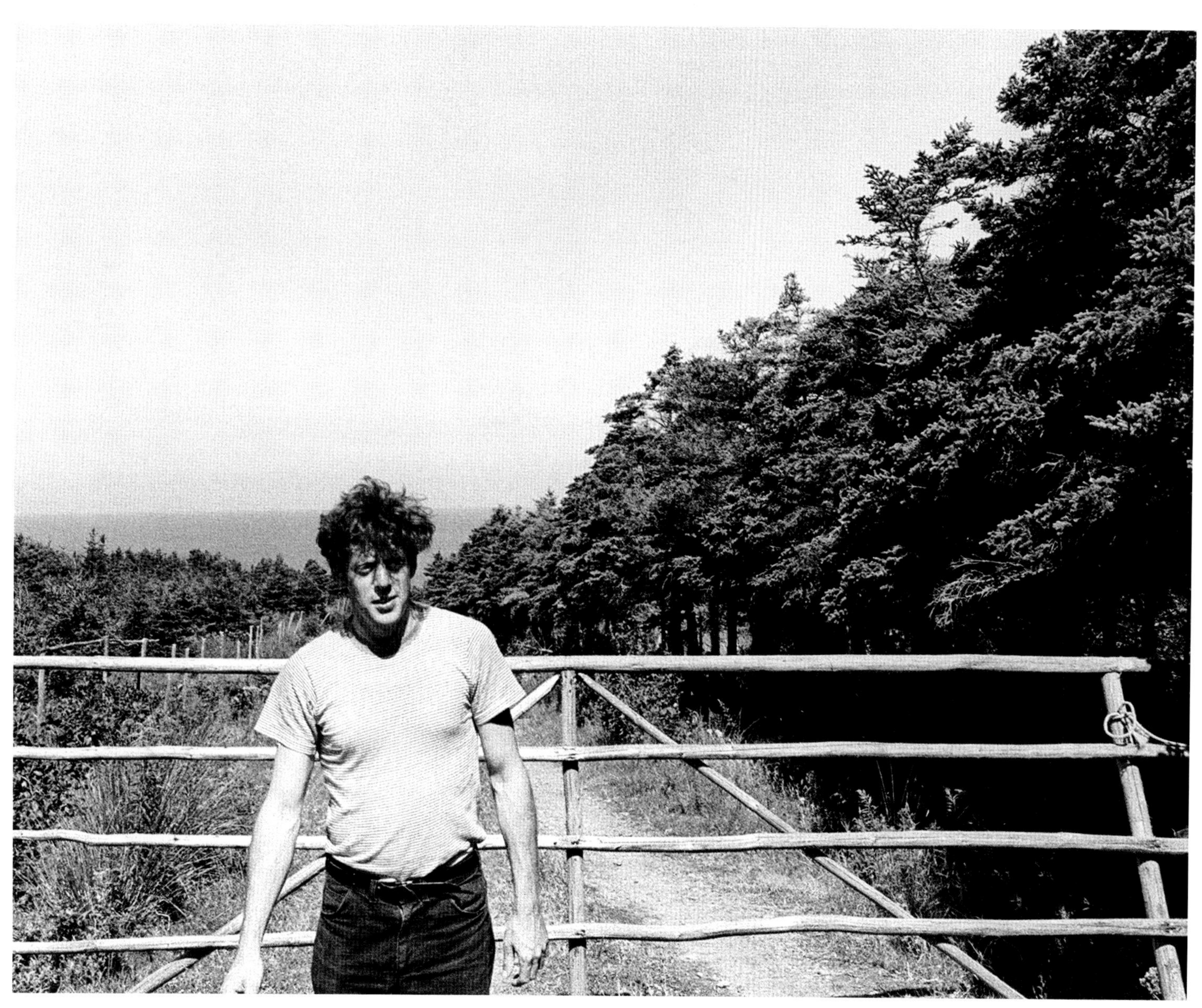

Philip Glass guarding the gate

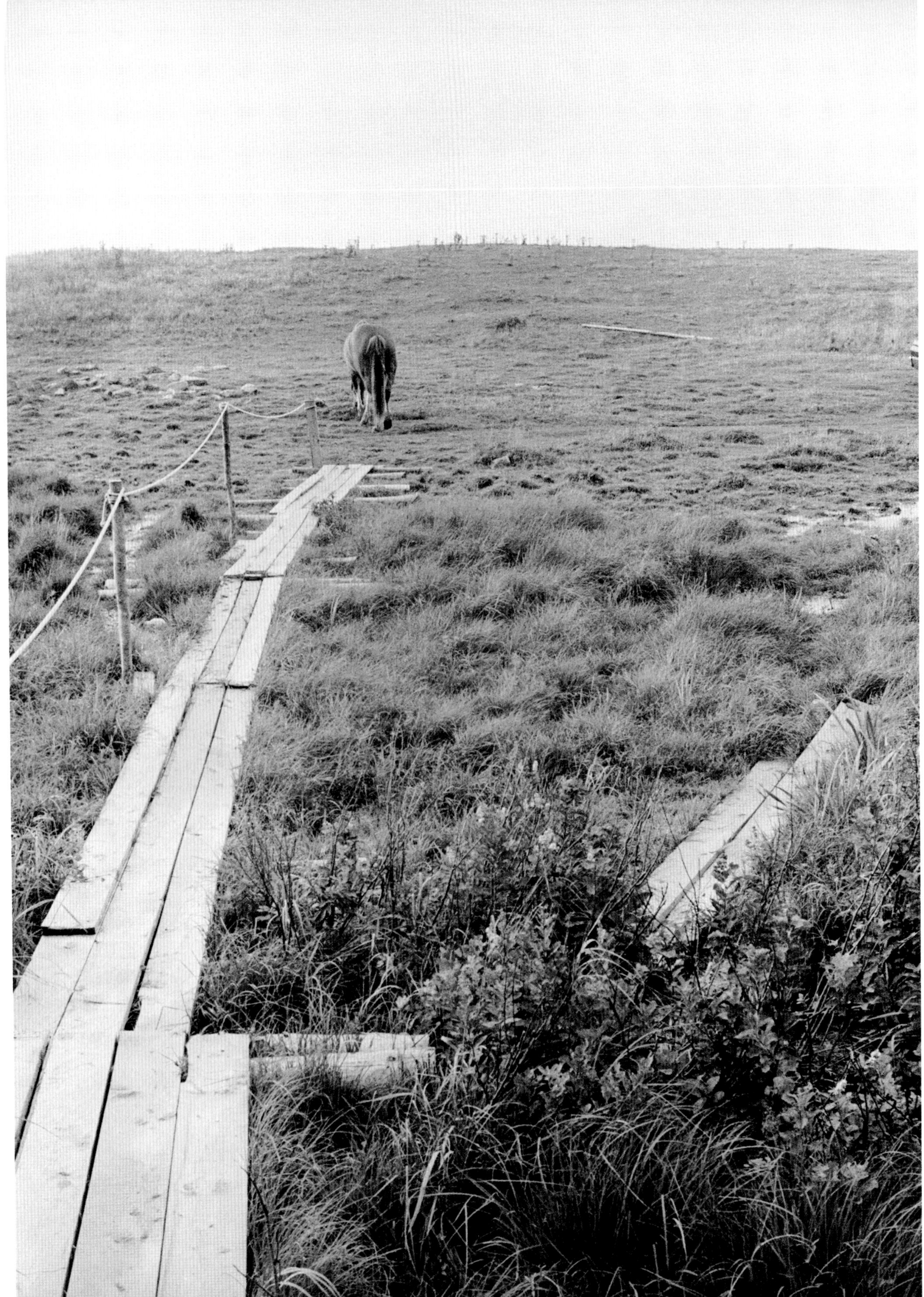

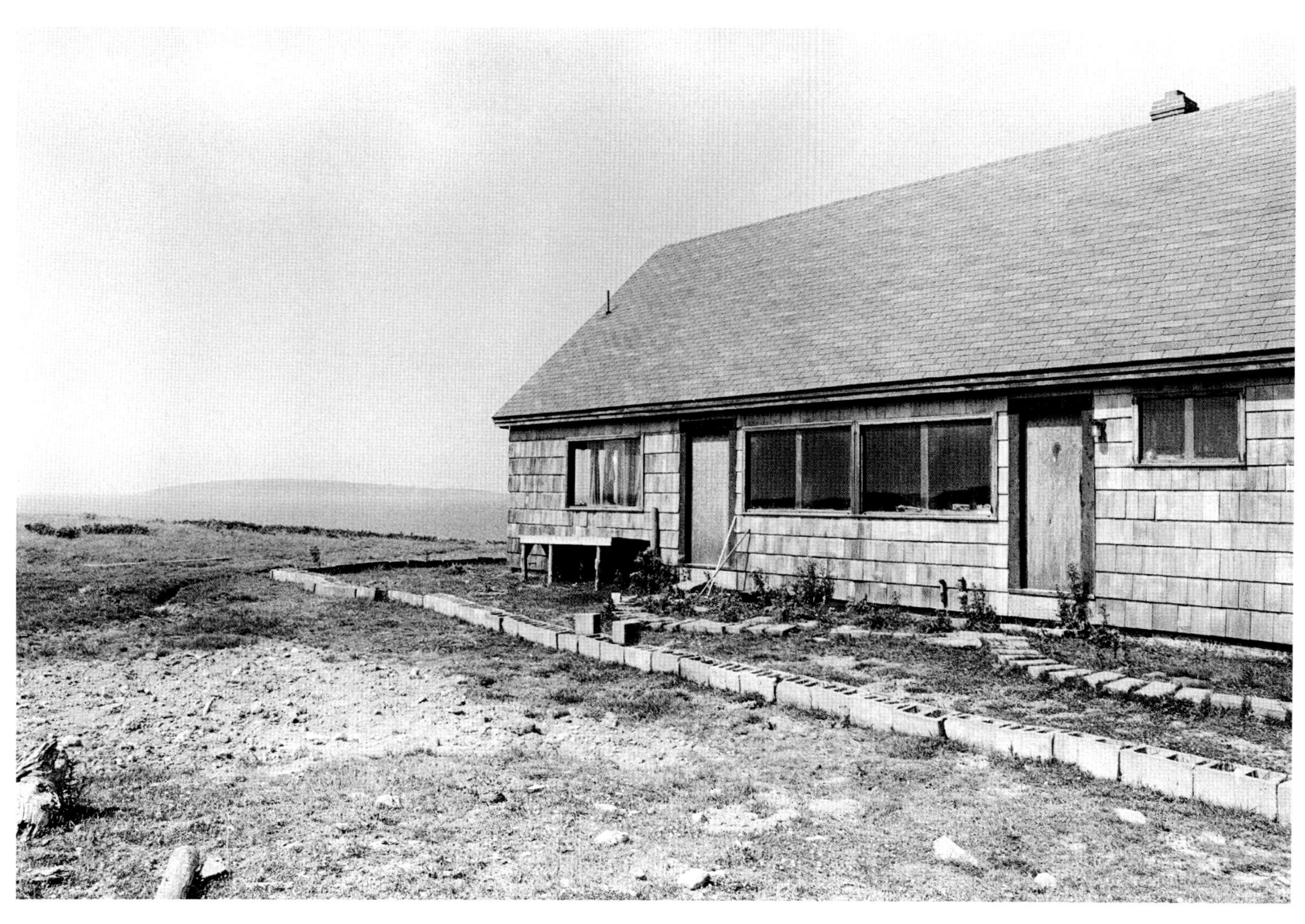

above, The Big House

left, Walkway across the marsh

Philip Glass and I went searching for a summer house to share that would allow us to escape the dense grid of summer life in the city. After a long journey, we finally arrived in Nova Scotia. We ended up impulsively buying an abandoned hunting lodge on the western coast of Cape Breton Island that overlooked the Northumberland Strait, a vast stretch of sea known as The Big Empty. In back of the lodge, small A-frames were hidden between clusters of pine trees. Standing on one of the huge, rocky cliffs overlooking a wide beach, one could look for miles down an empty coast. It was a dramatic experience of sea, wind and sky that encouraged playfully spontaneous and impulsive release from art world ambitions and urban stress. Soon summers became longer and stretched into dramatic fall displays and what at first seemed to be a brief vacation became a location that offered not only escape but also interior journeys into work and self-discovery.

Rudy Wurlitzer

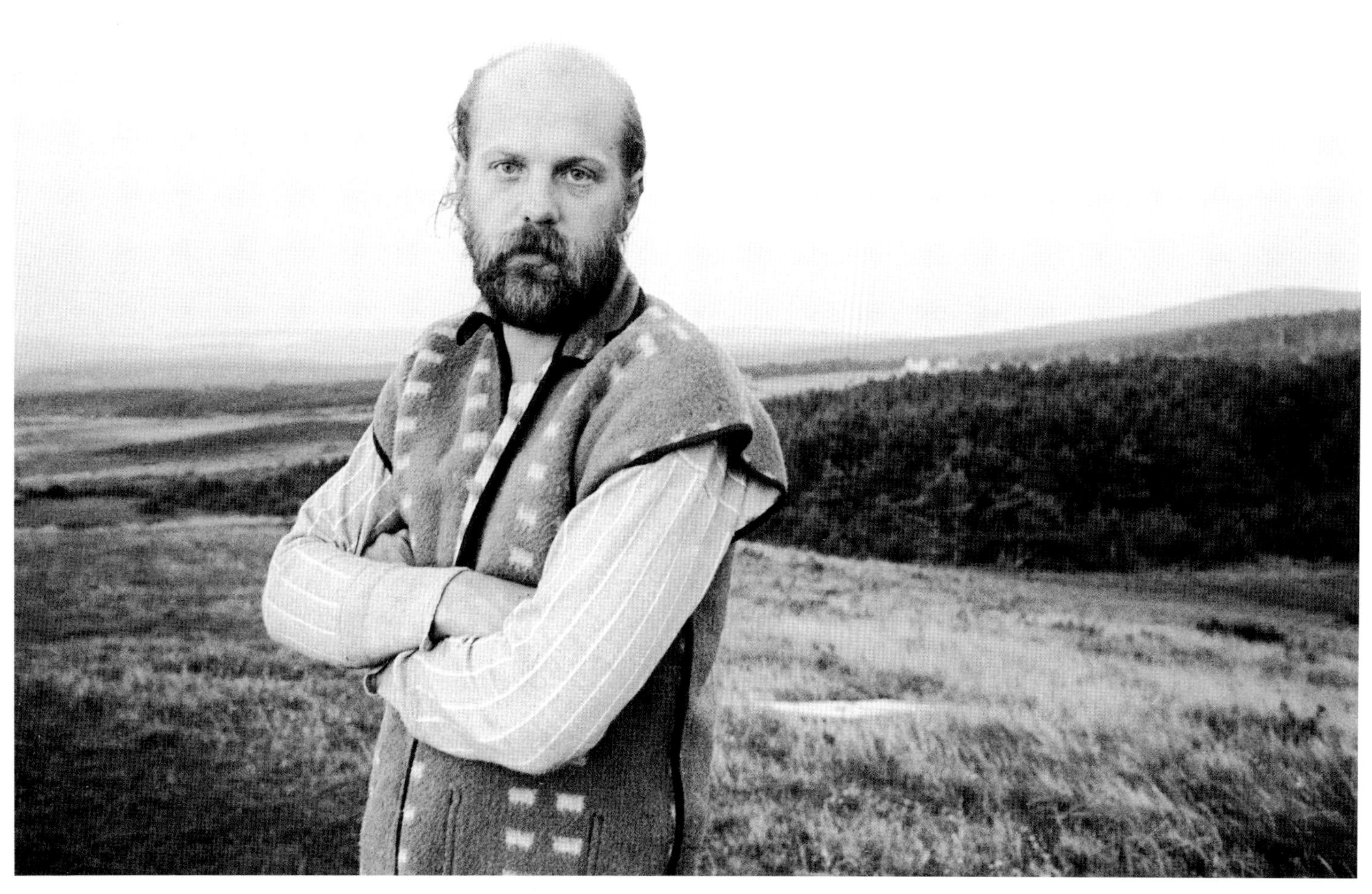

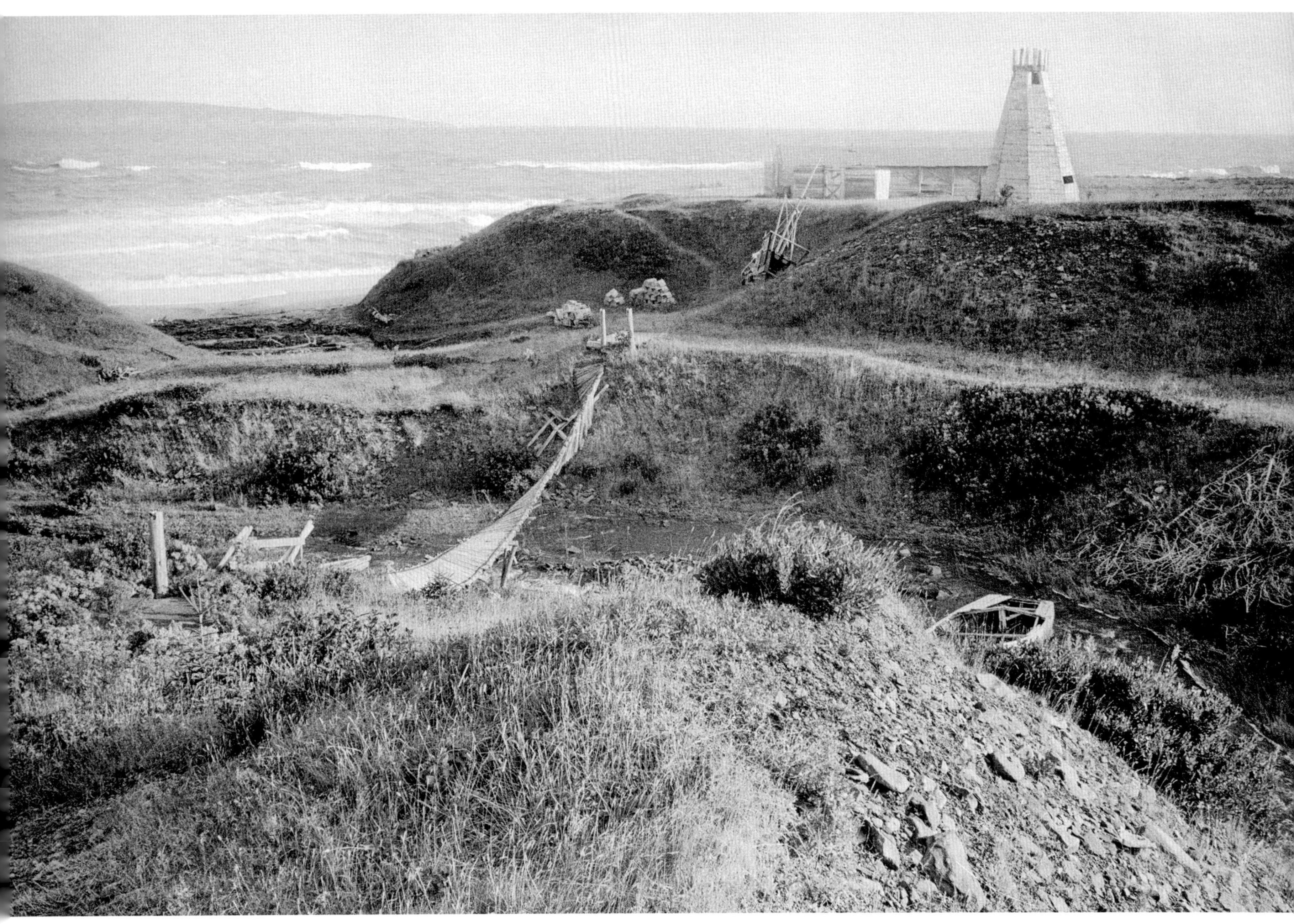

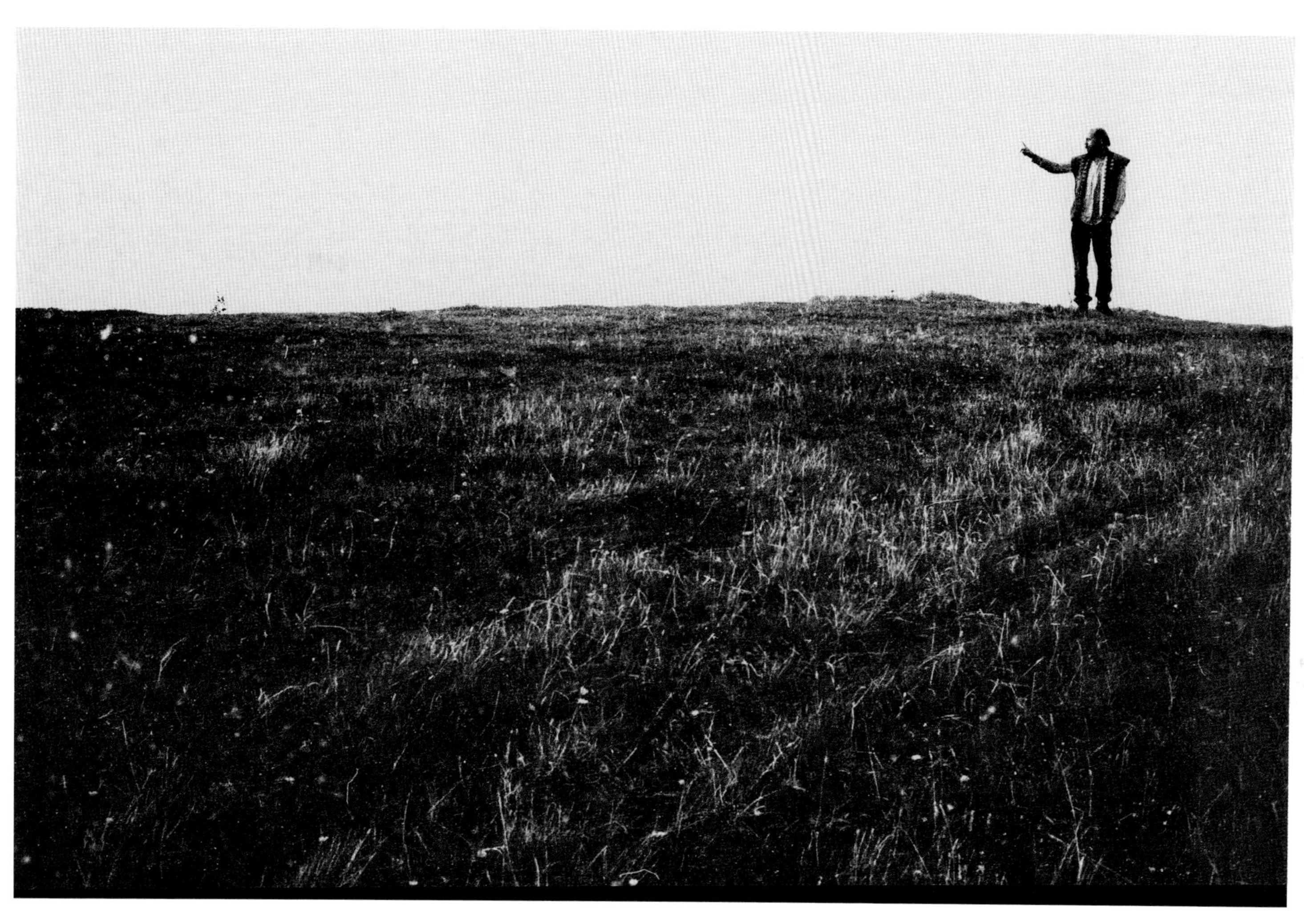

above, Rudy

left, Ancient path to empty beaches

You don't see the house from the Shore Road, or even when you turn into the sprucey "driveway" over the little wooden creek bridge, through beautiful woods where a few A-frame cabins begin to appear and then down a trough, up a little hill, and there it is, surprisingly grand in an odd way... "The Big House," a blue roofed, grey shingled, many windowed, long building near a cliff, looking out at the vast sea and the rising gentle slope of Margaree Island."

JoAnne Akalaitis

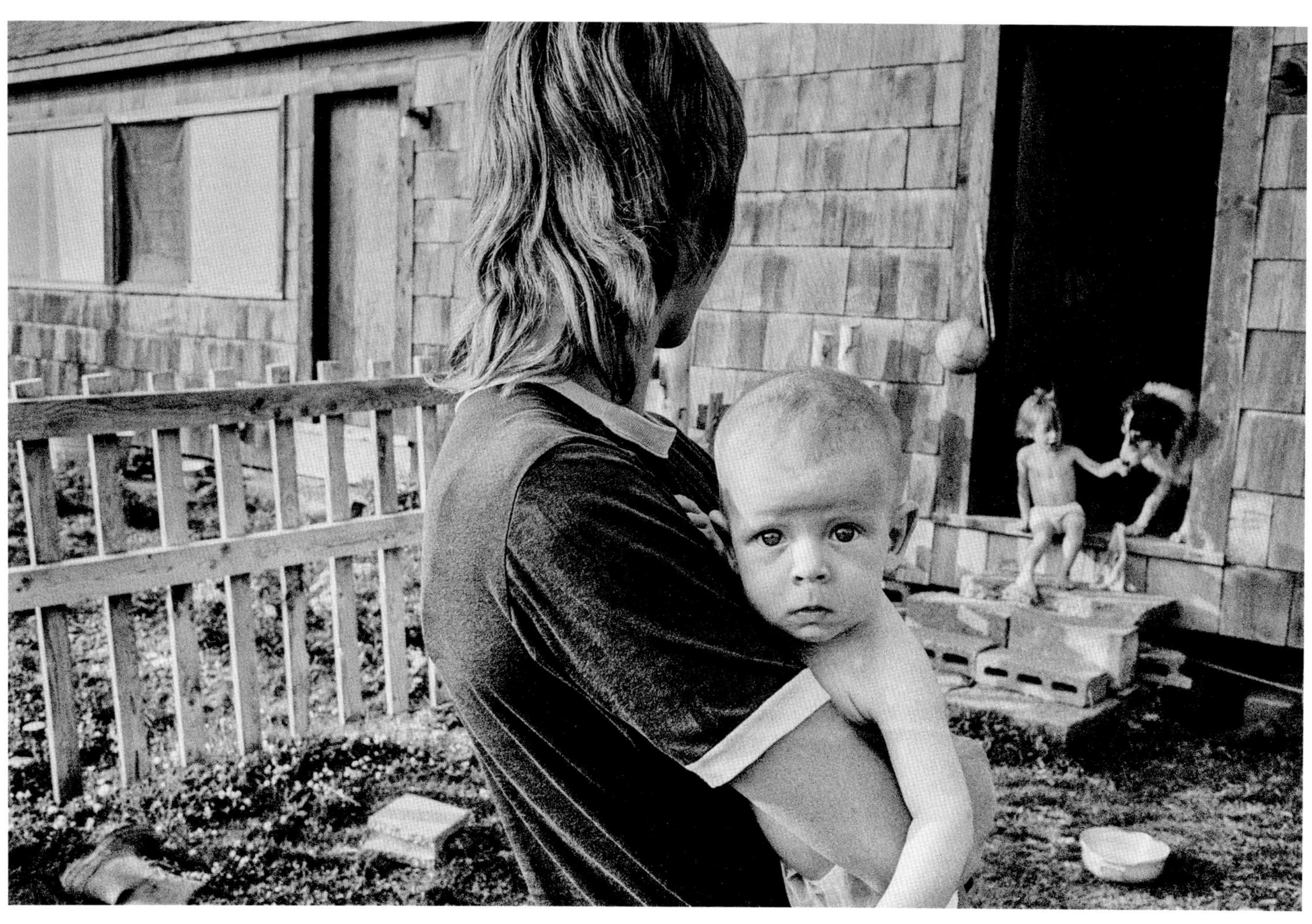

JoAnne with Zack, Juliet and Joey

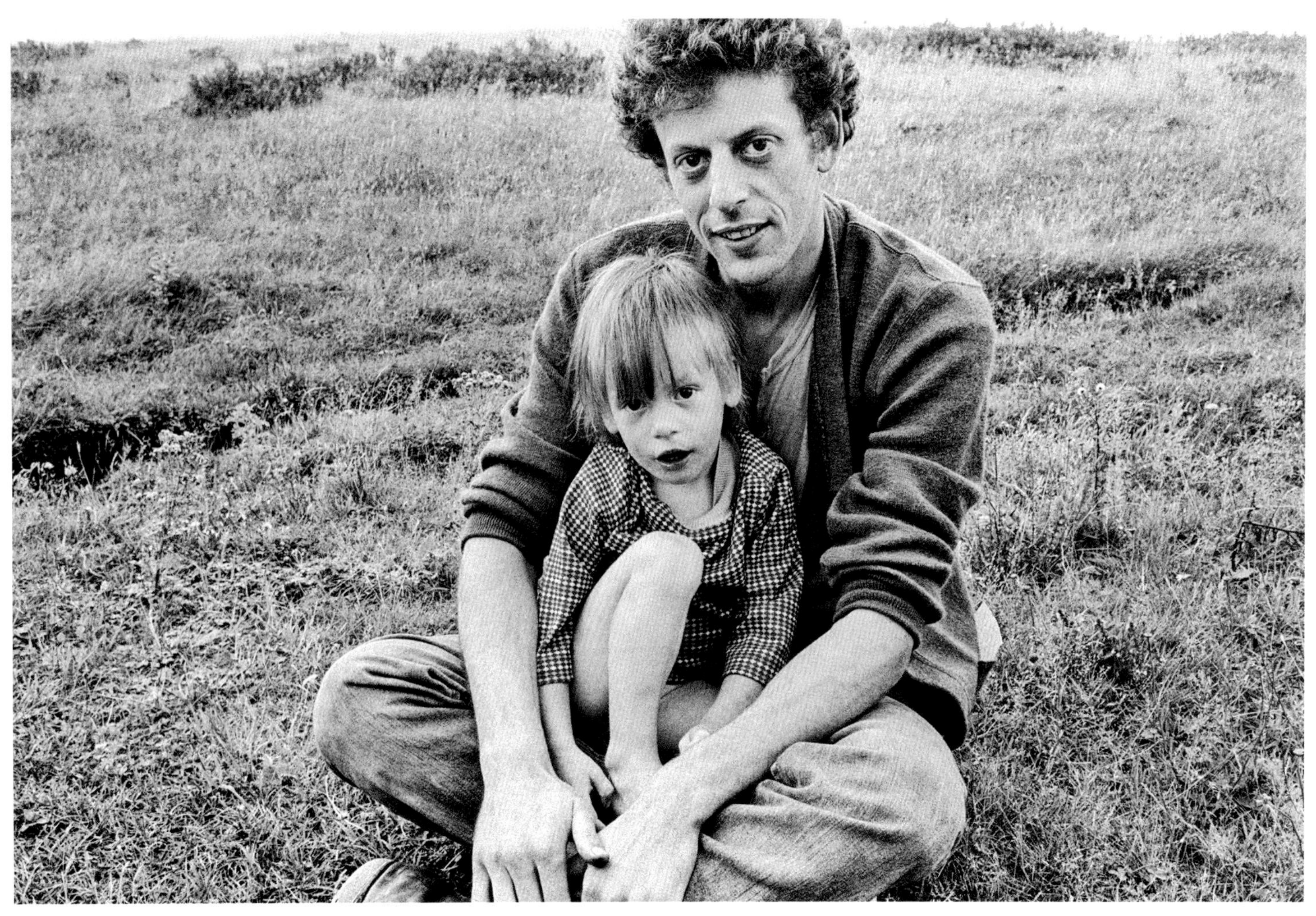

above, Philip with Juliet

right, Philip and Juliet on the beach with neighbors

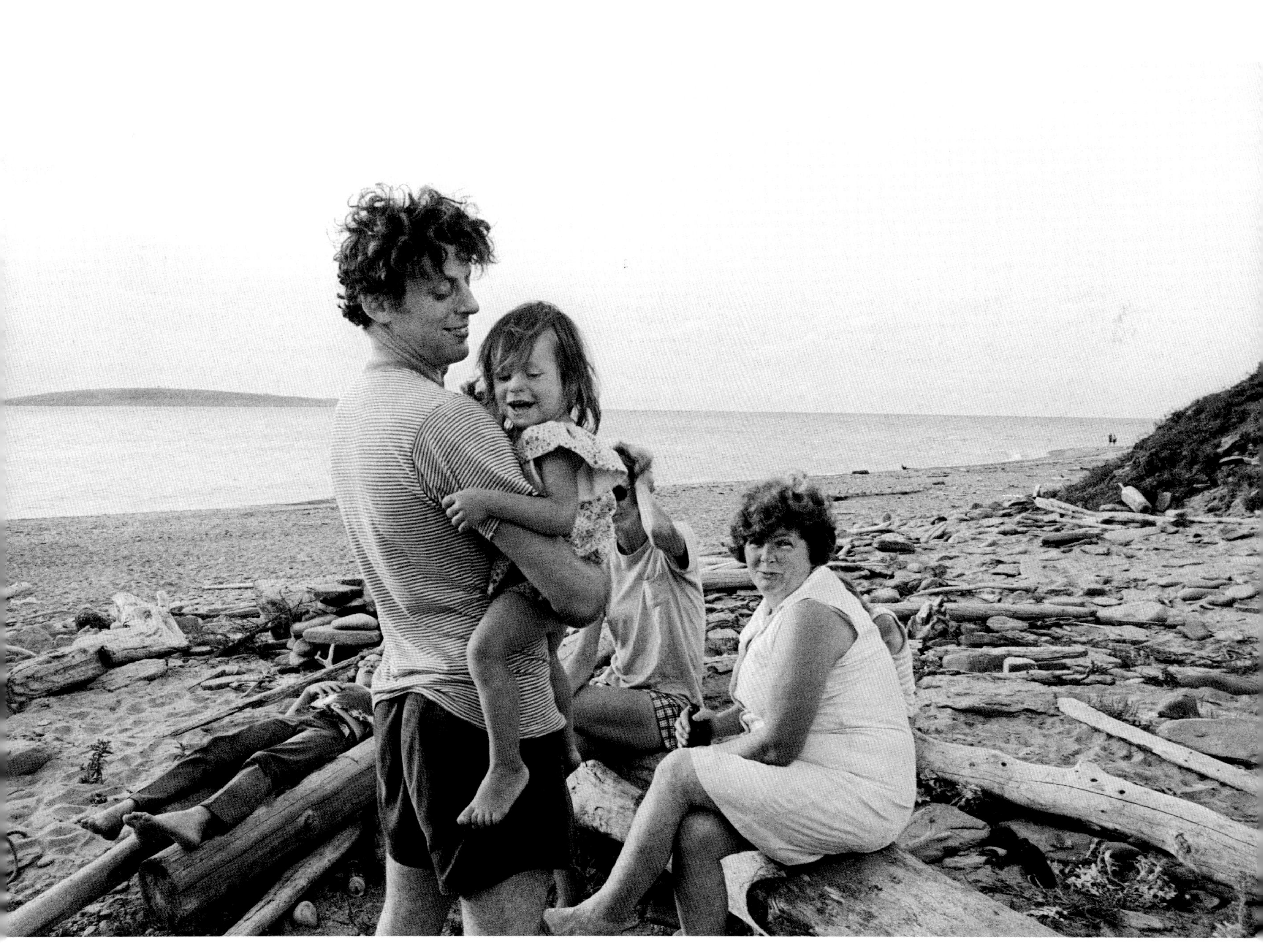

Many things seemed to come together in this place, and it felt like I just somehow fit in. If I were to say what most impressed me from my summers in Cape Breton, it would have to be the sense of friendliness and creativity that existed between these people, their art, and their strong connection to the natural landscape.

Greg Neiman

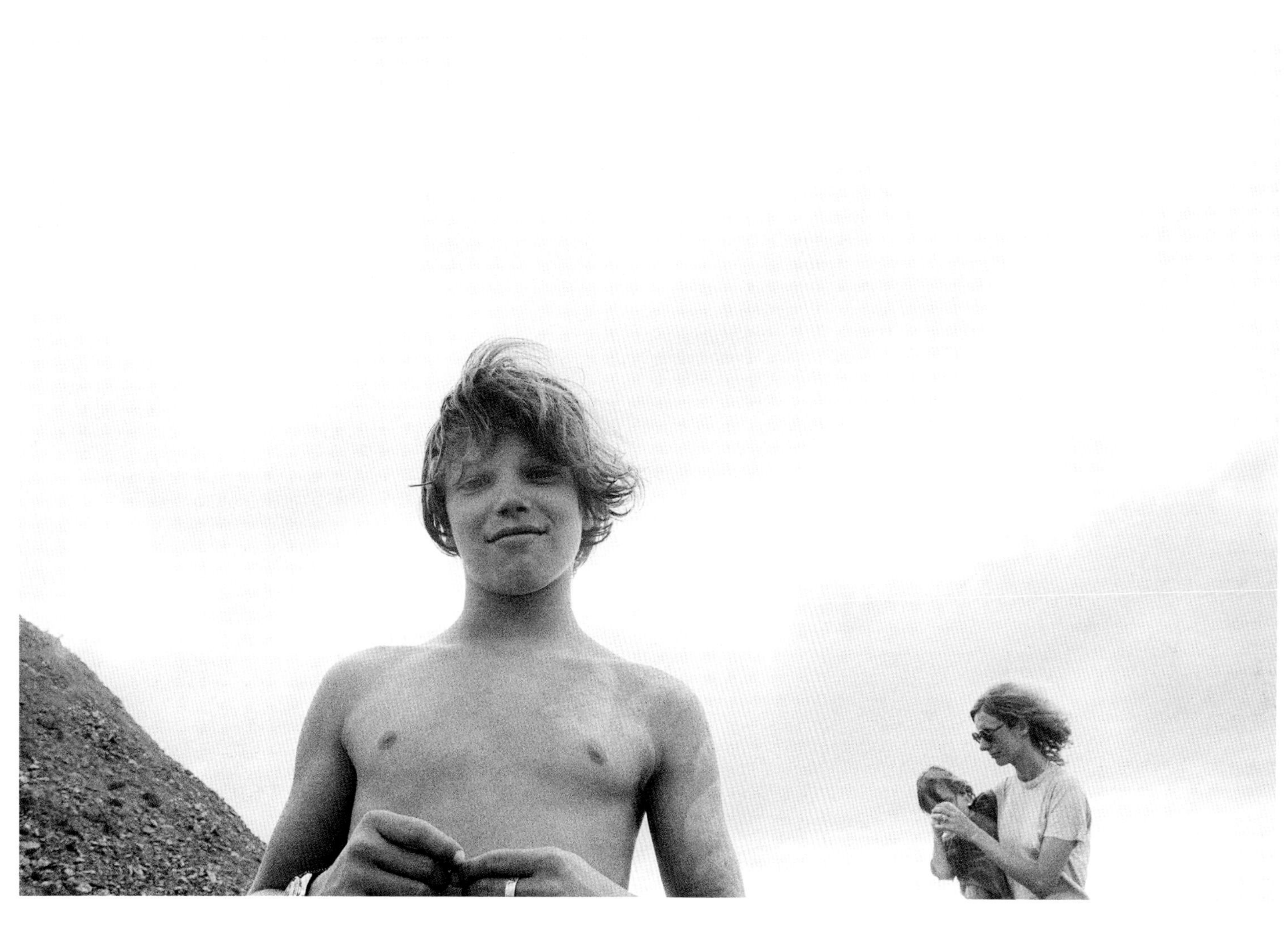

Greg with JoAnne and Juliet

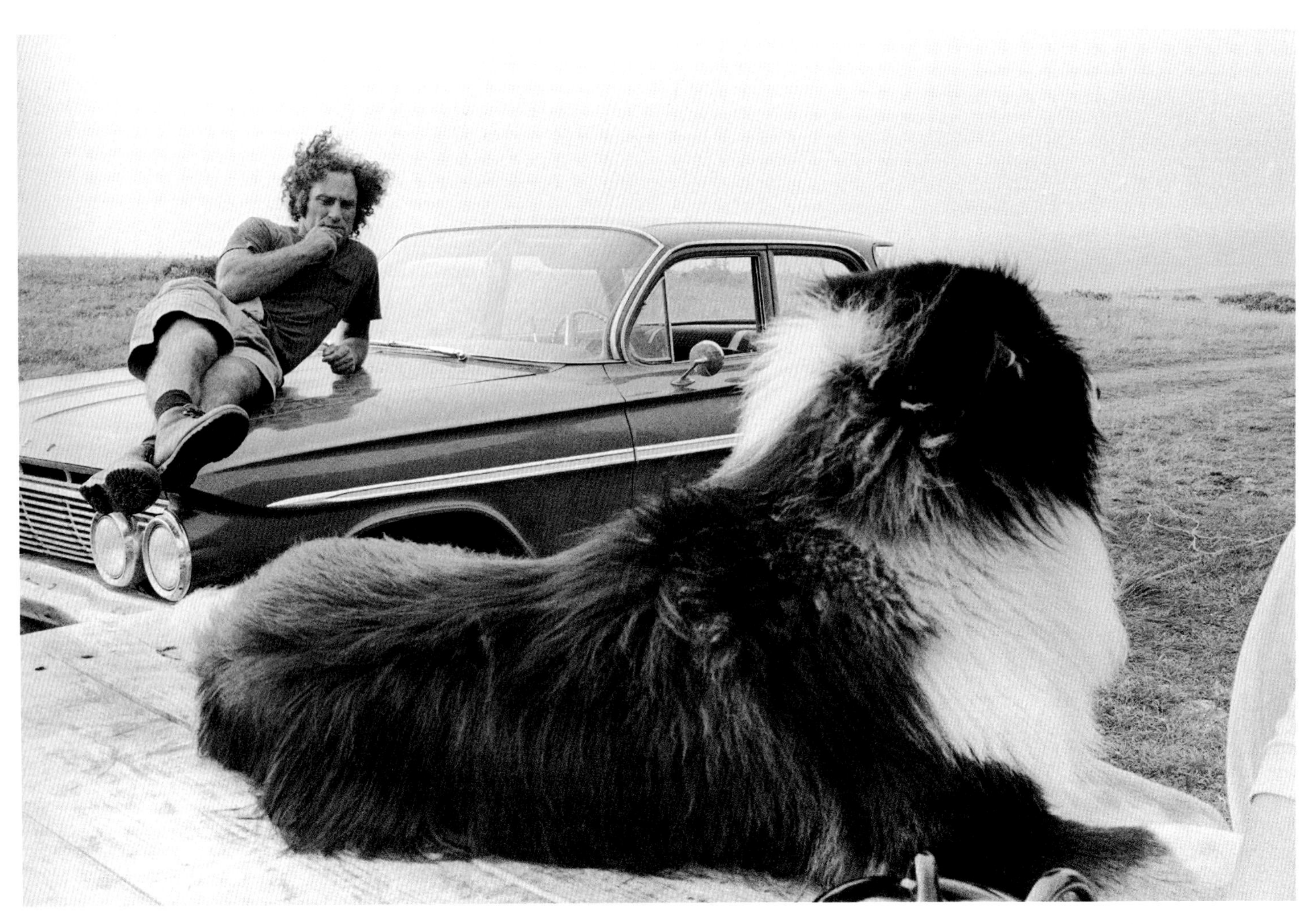

above, Richard with Joey

right, Rudy with Joey

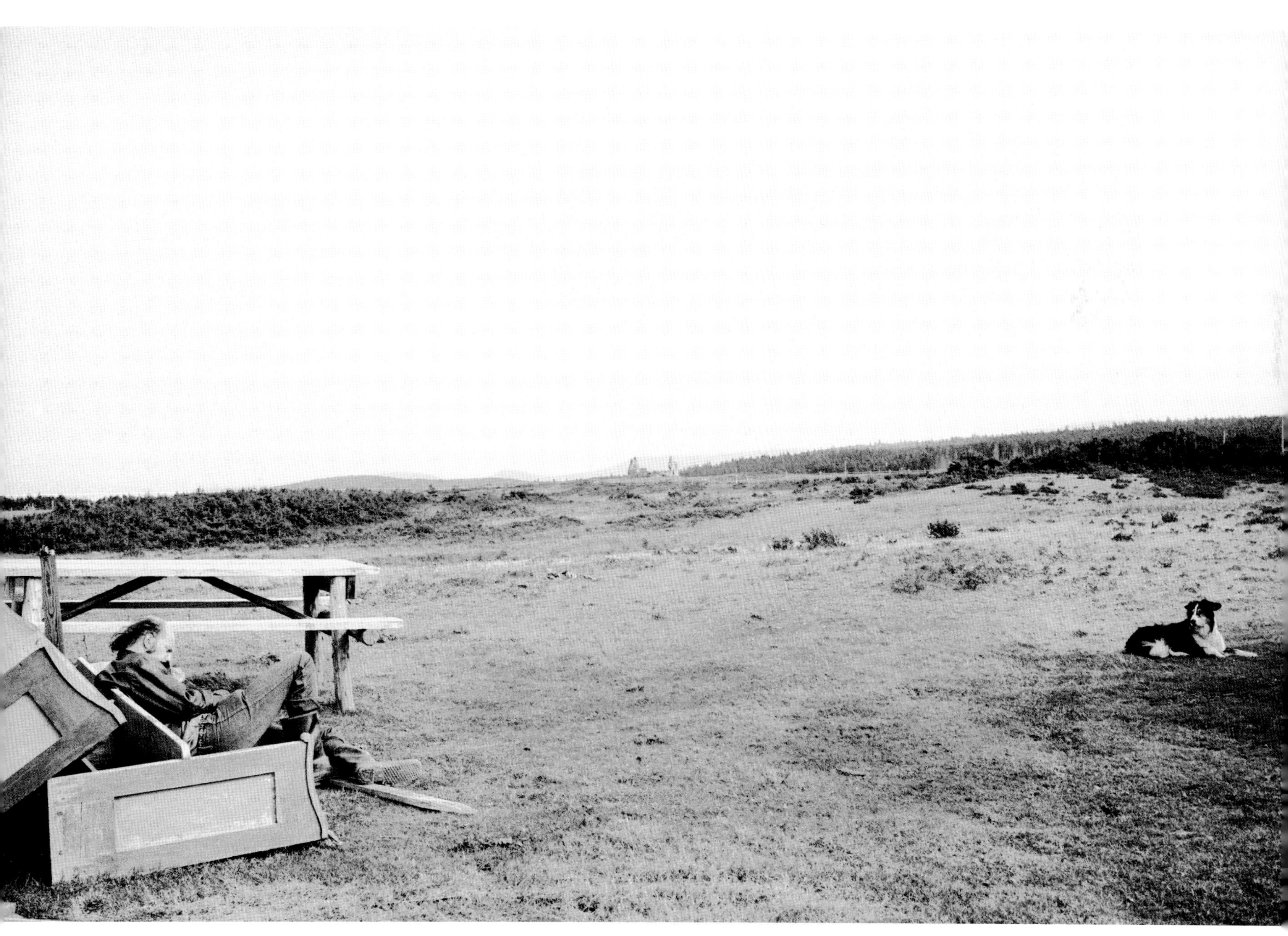

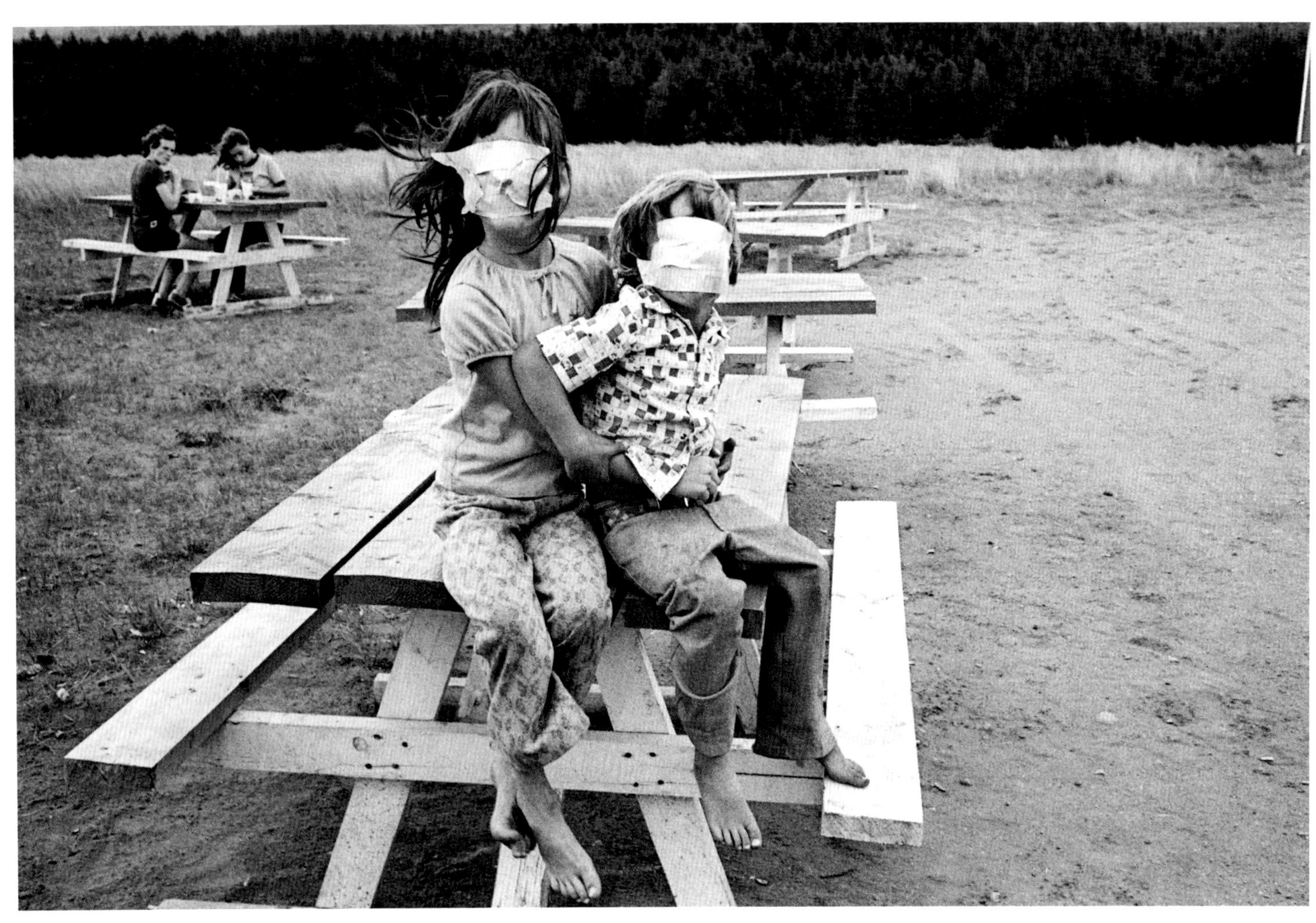

Picnics and playtime

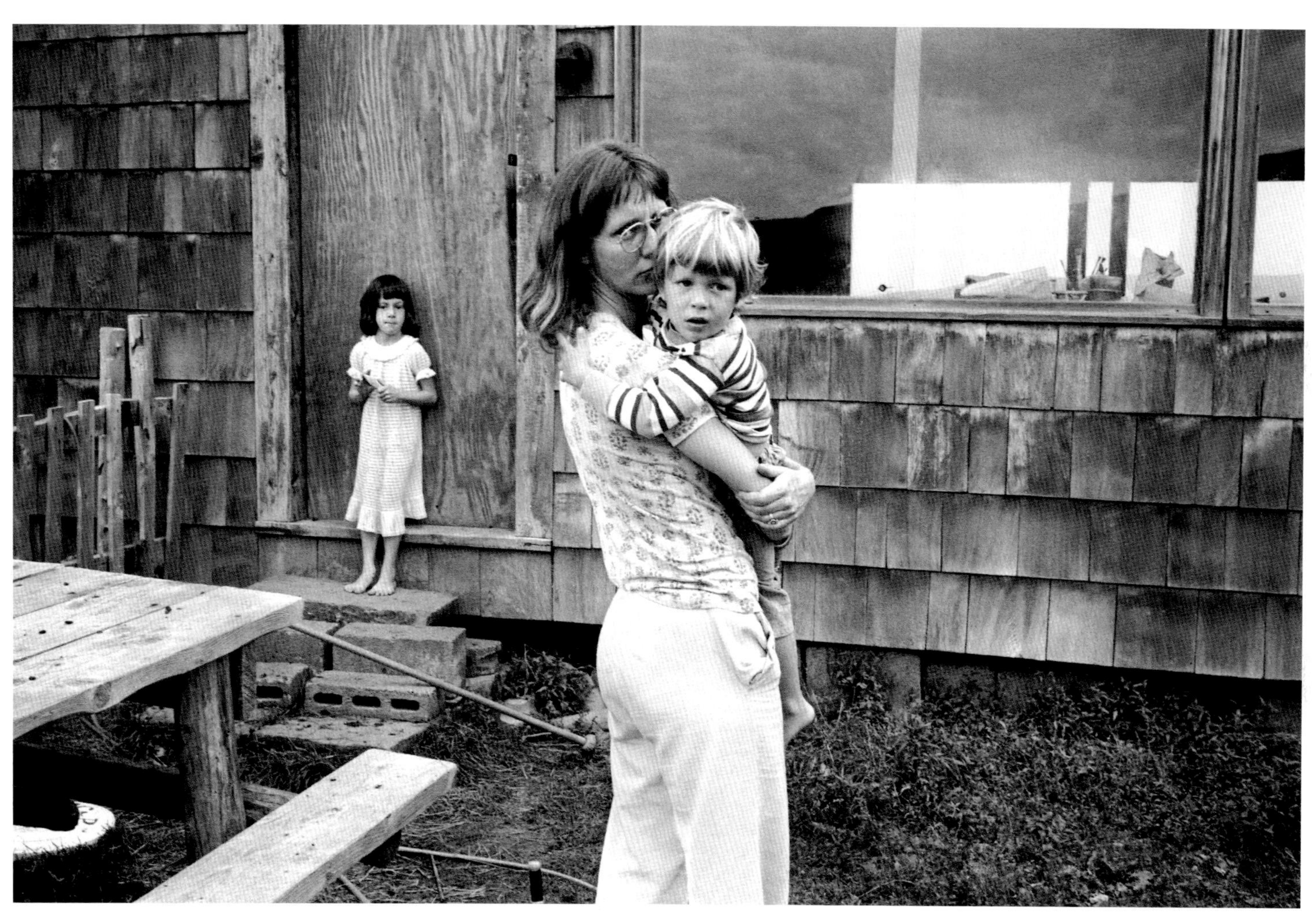

JoAnne with Zack and Juliet

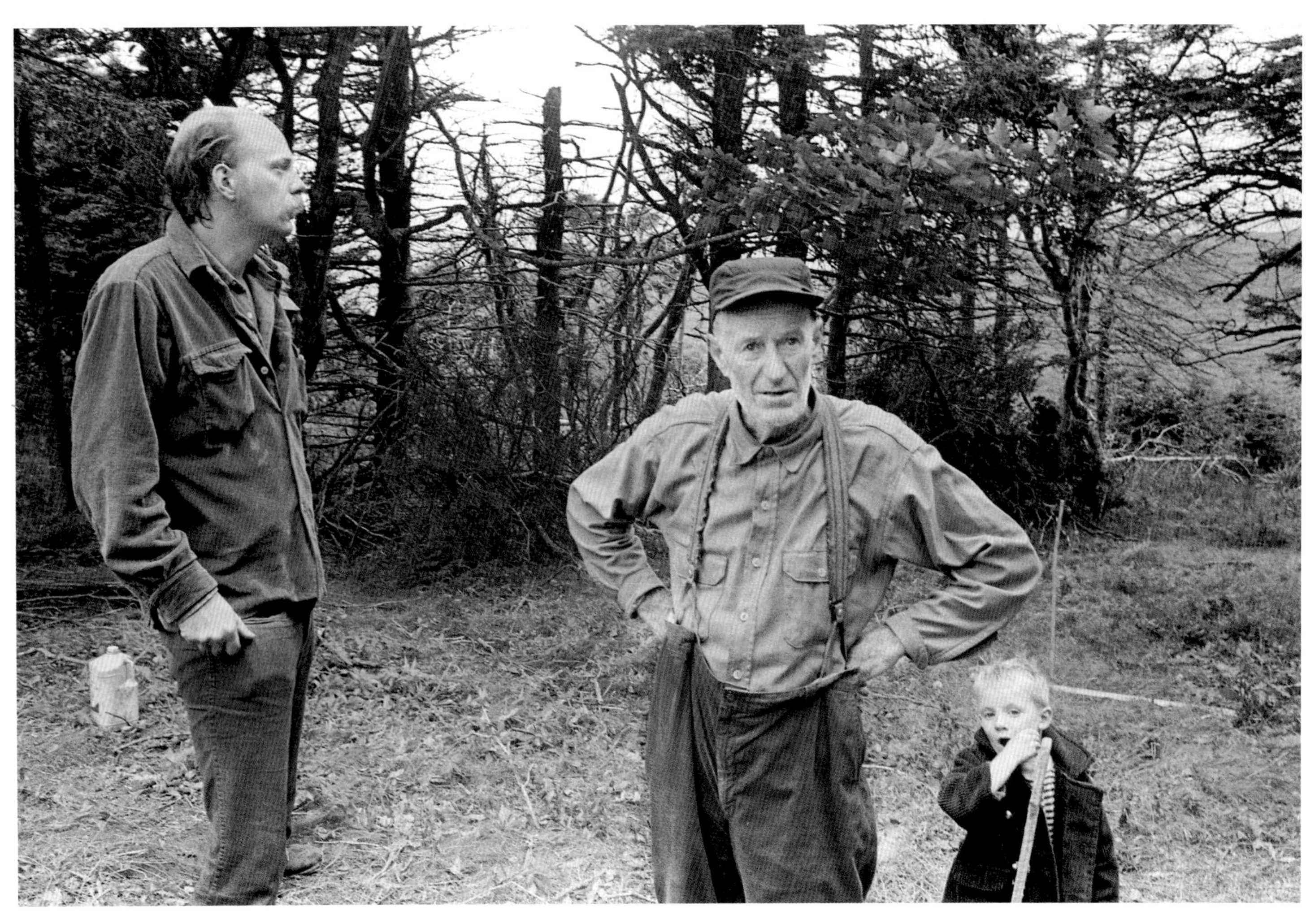

Rudy and John-Dan survey the land

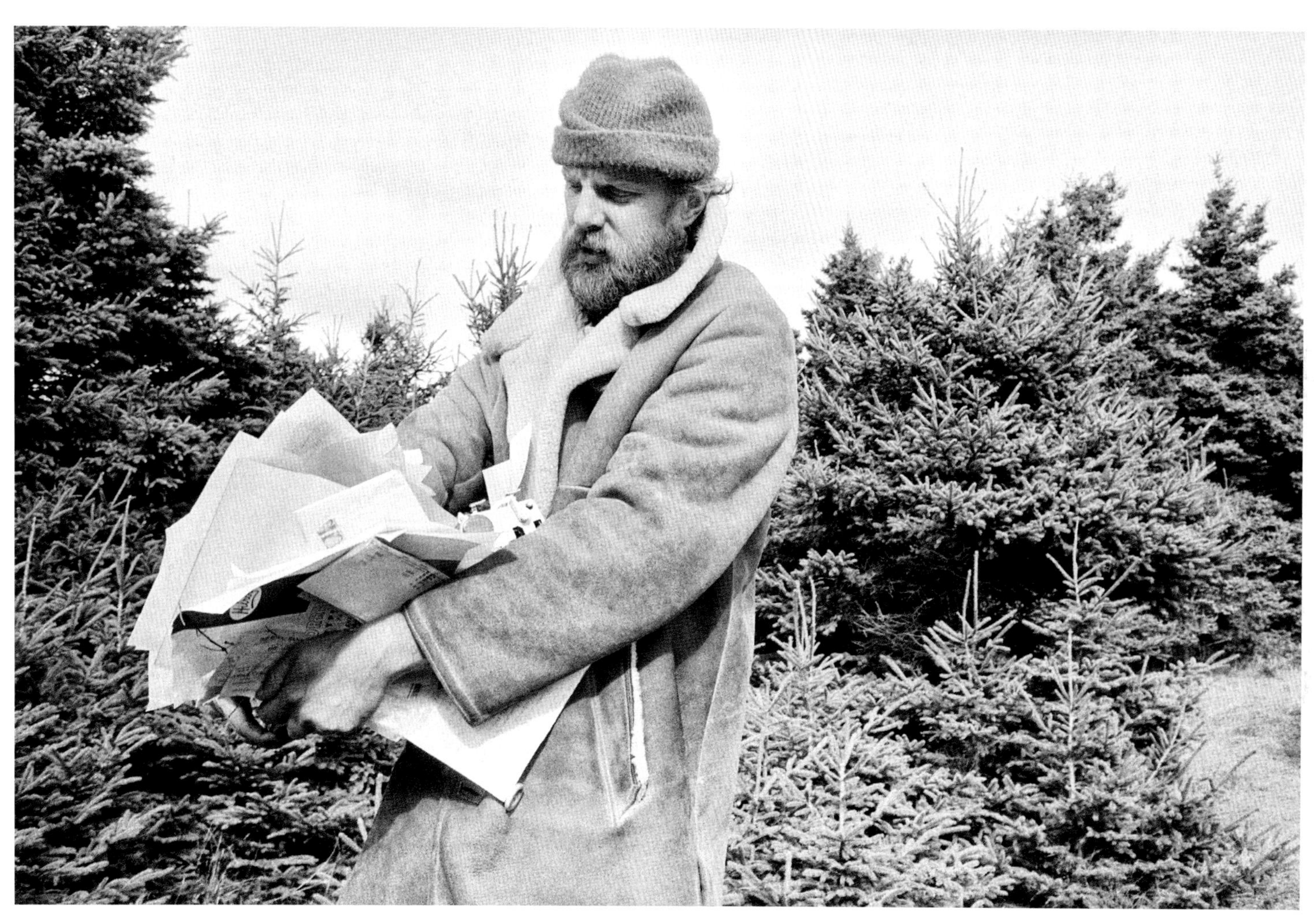

Rudy moving his office

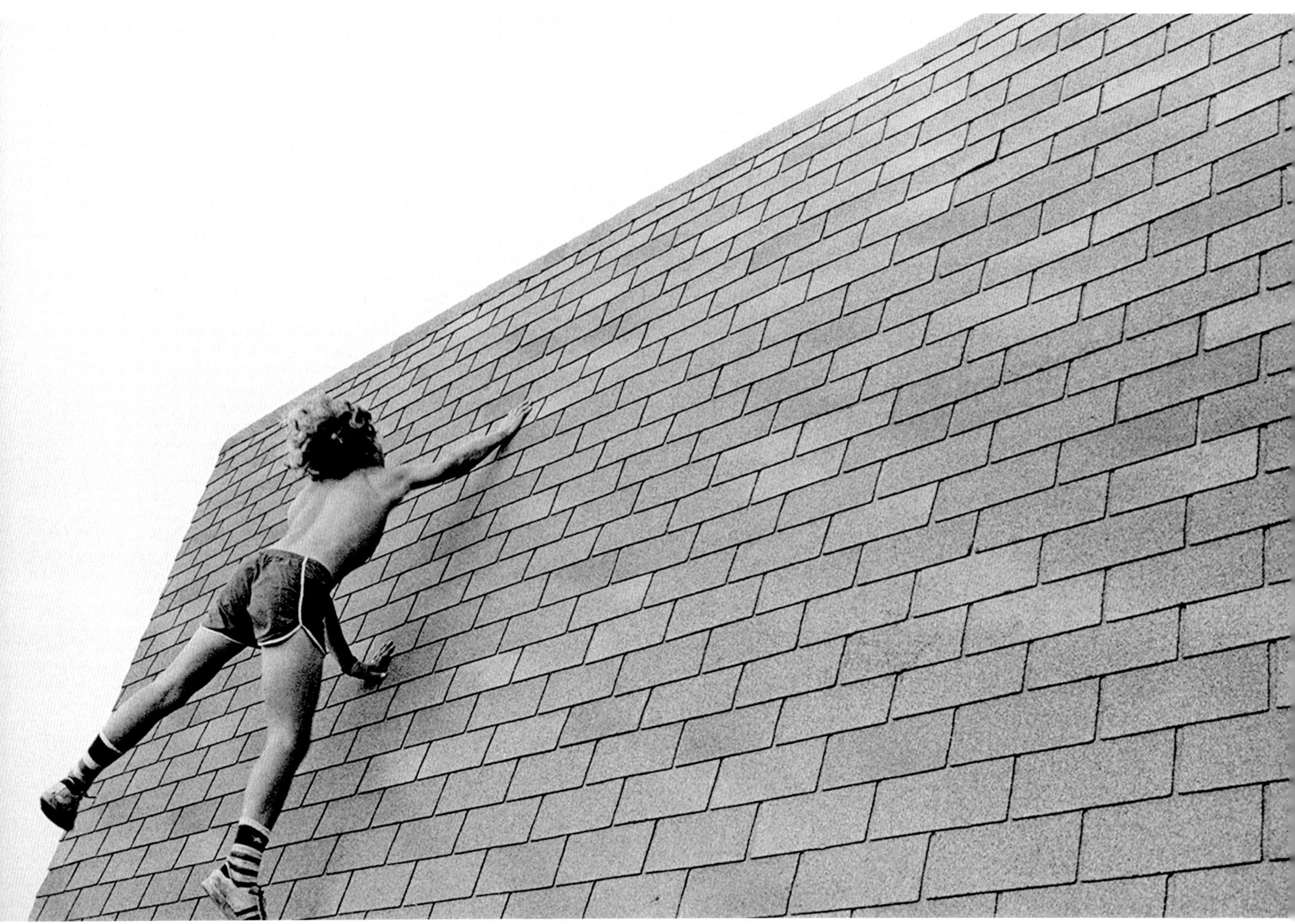

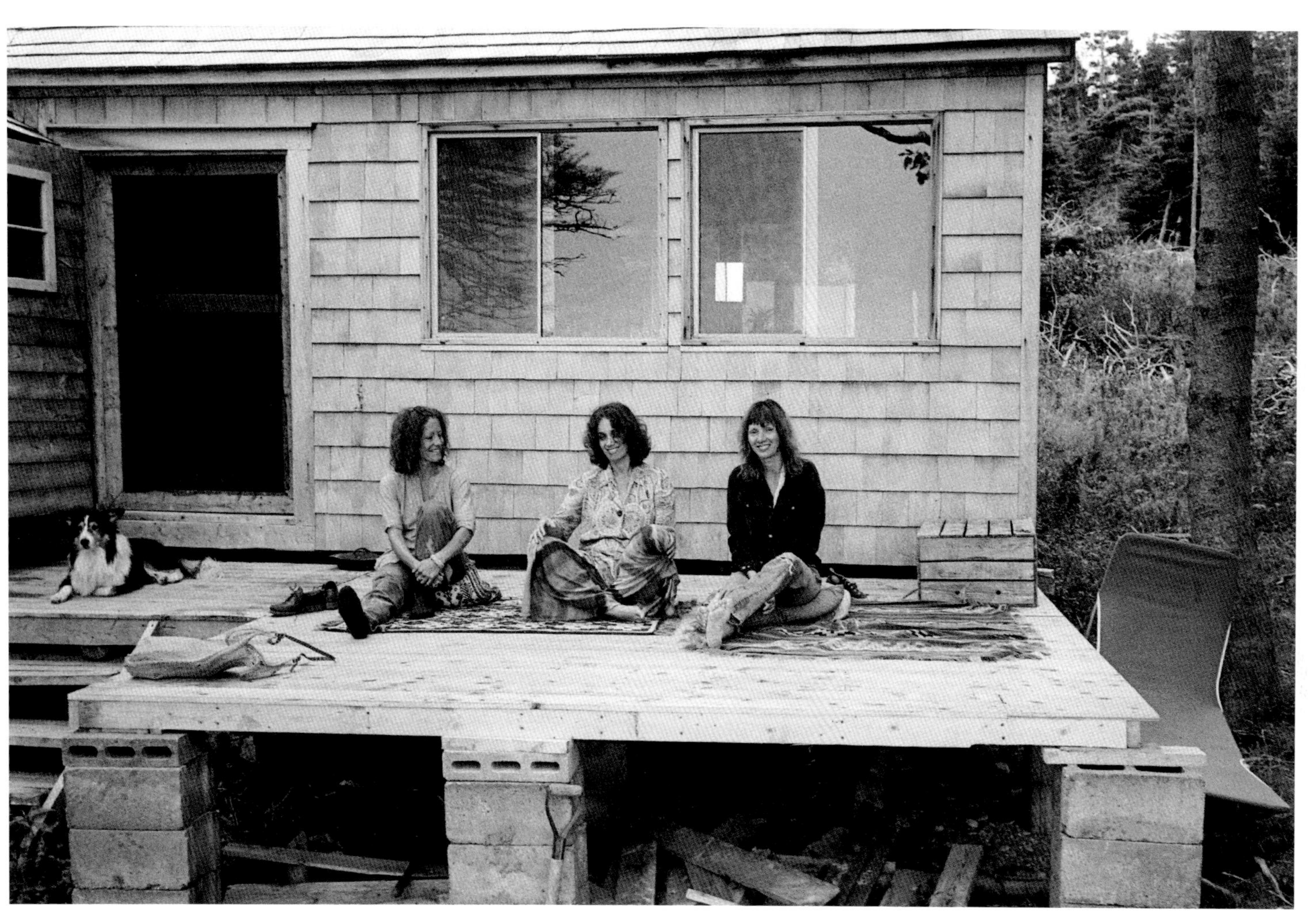

above, Joan Jonas, Roberta and JoAnne

left, Greg makes the winning leap

The Big House: scene of hanging out, playing Gordon Lightfoot and Beatles' records, big communal dinners, dance parties, birthday parties, Phil's ensemble rehearsals, yoga, enormous space for kids to play, Juliet and Zachary, Ruth and Lee's daughter, Roberta's son Greg, the three Katz kids, and the amazing MacPherson family from next door, seventeen of them. They showed up the first day we arrived, and I was amazed as one by one they trickled around and into the house and I realized they were all from the same family. I got pregnant the first summer with Zack and remember making curries, exacerbating morning sickness, plus meetings with Pat Katz and Ruth about how best to feed the kids nutritiously on our tiny budget.

JoAnne Akalaitis

Family portrait

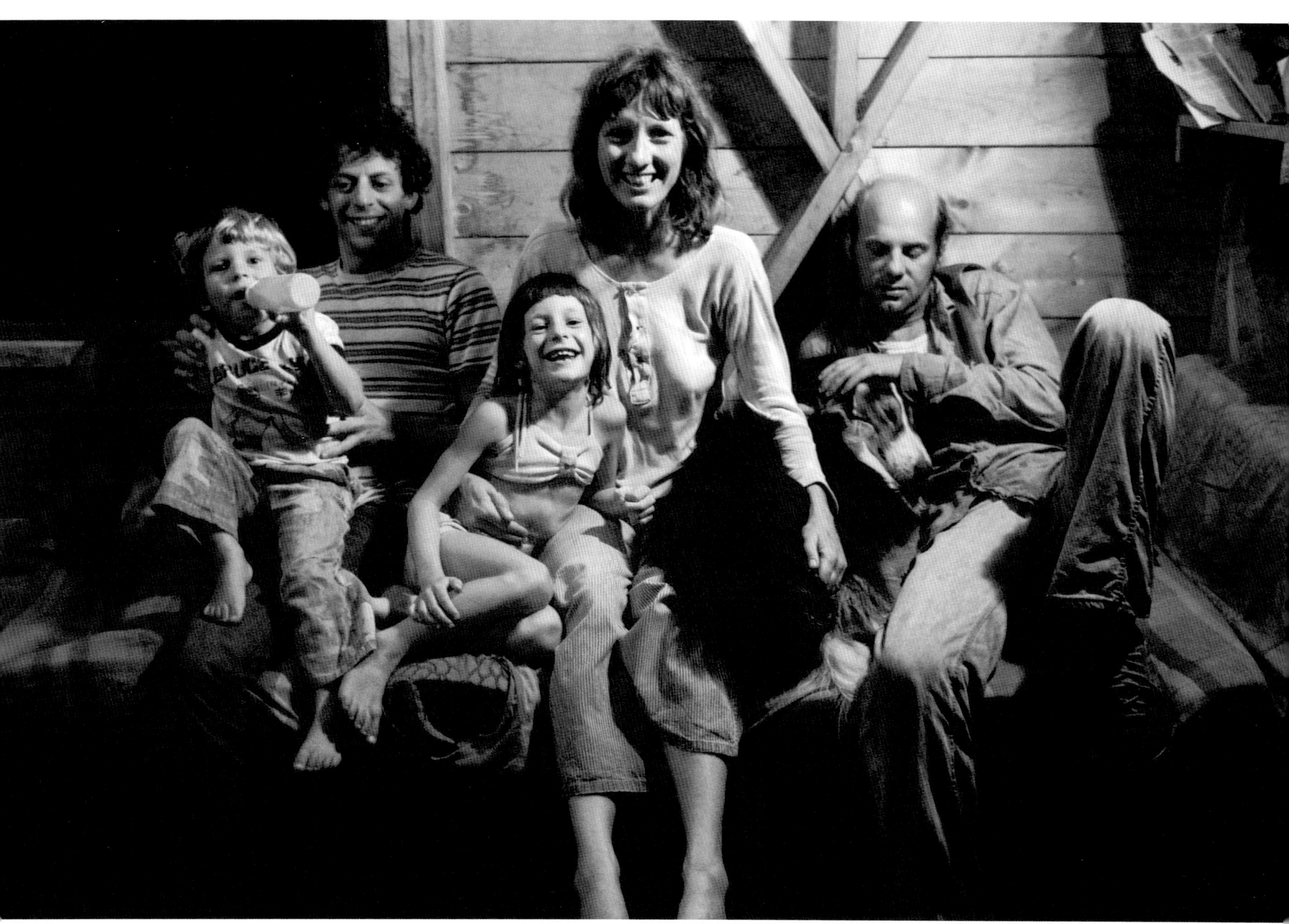

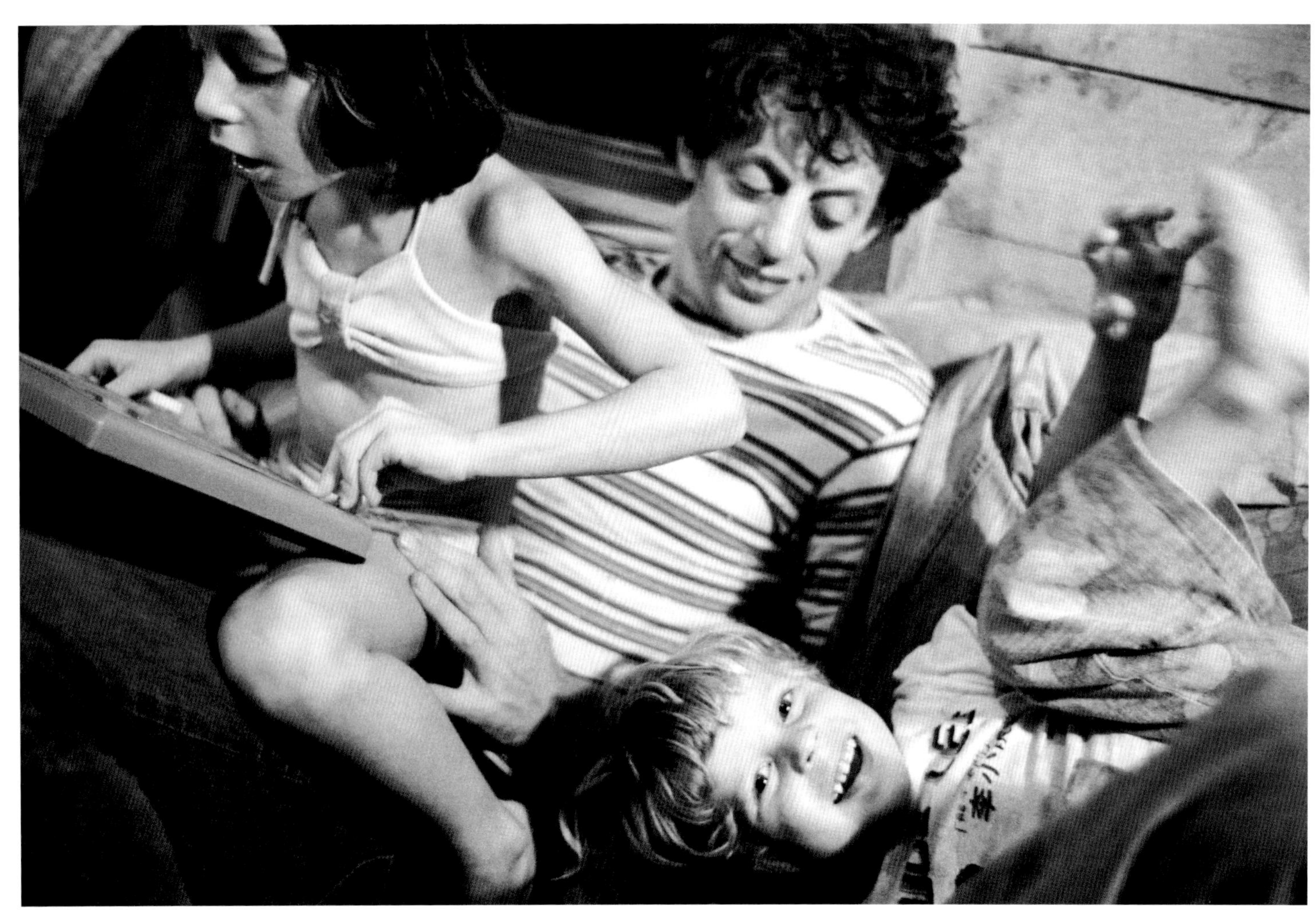

Philip with his kids

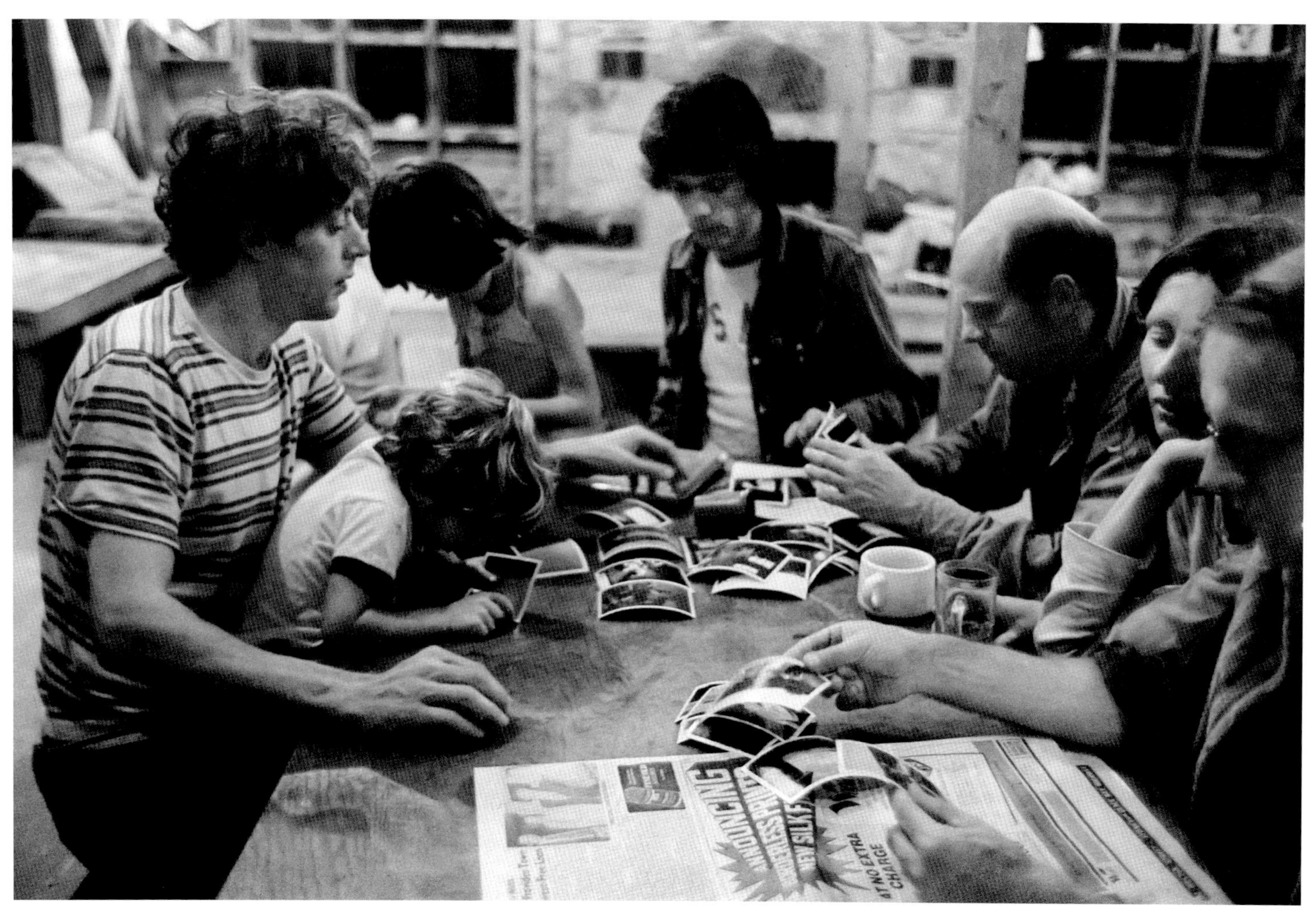

Group critique in The Big House

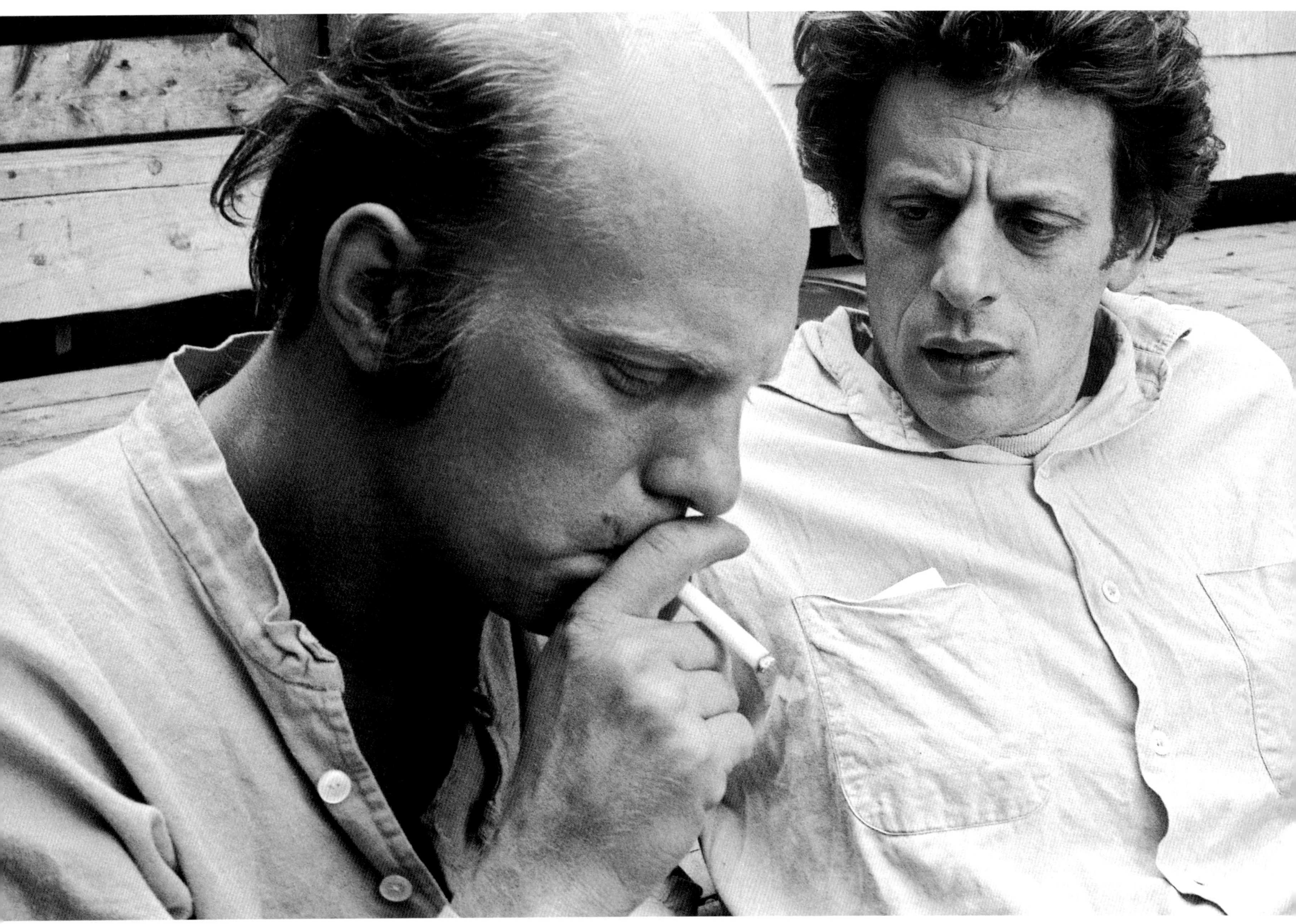

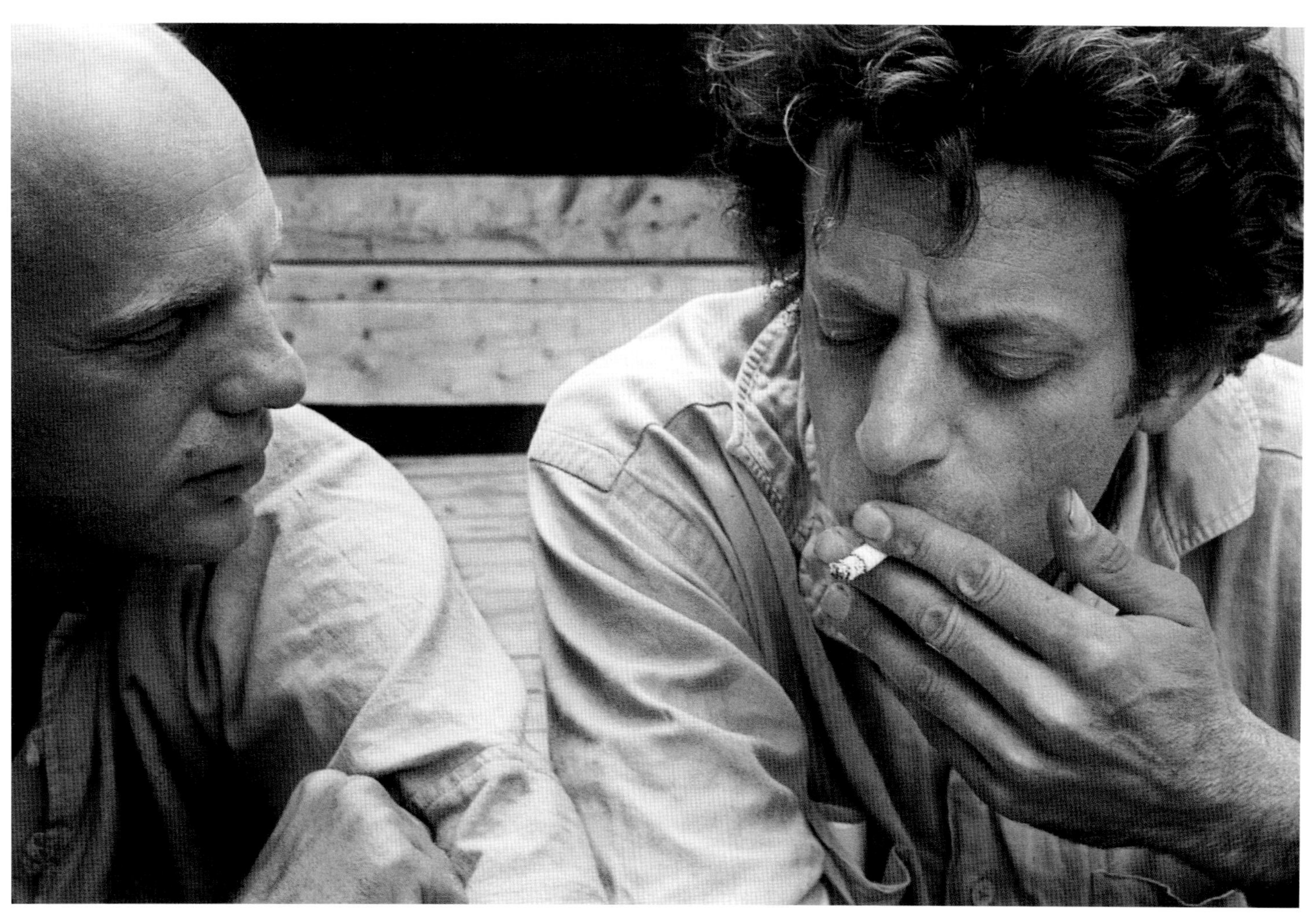

Scheming and dreaming

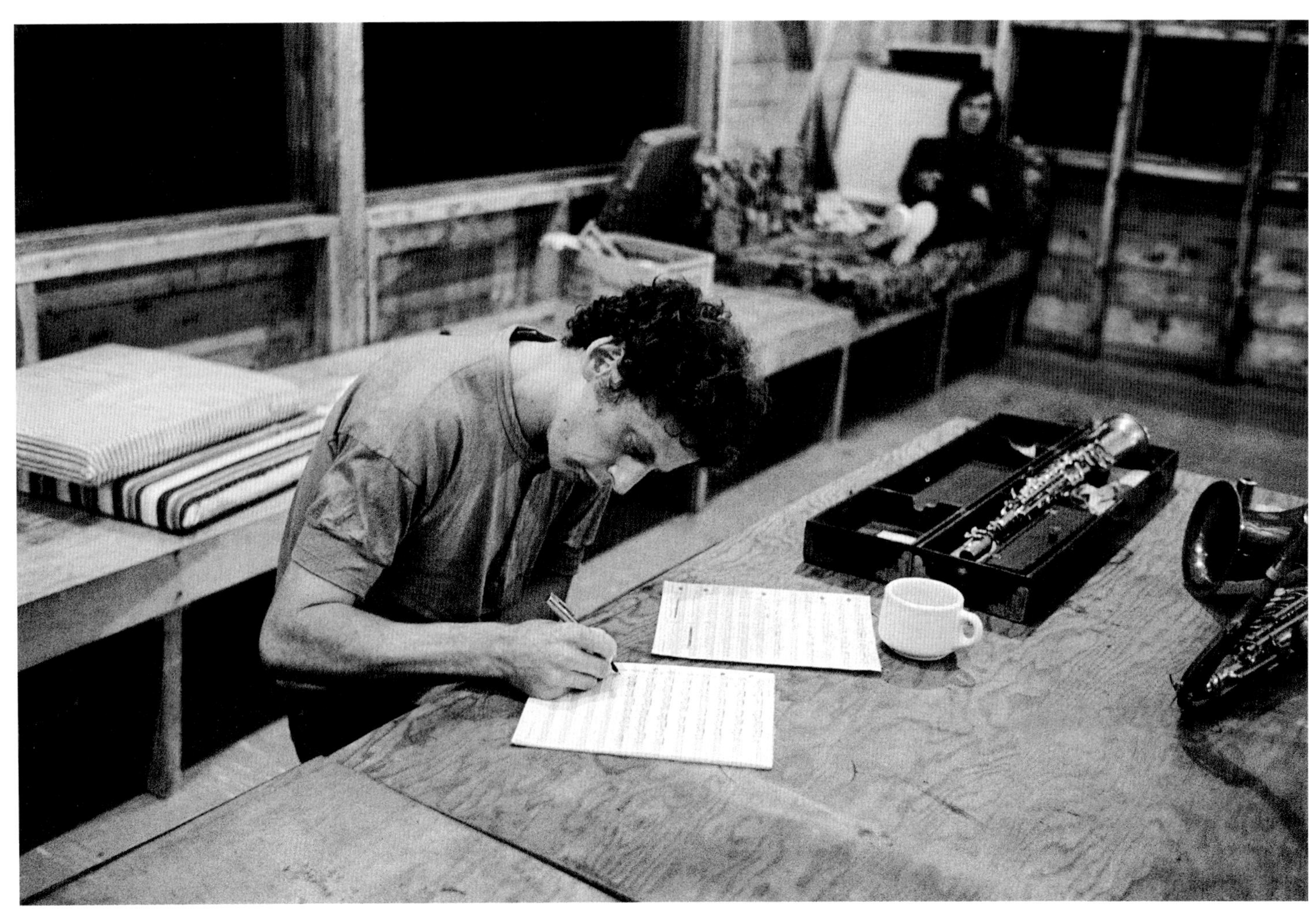

Philip and Dickie

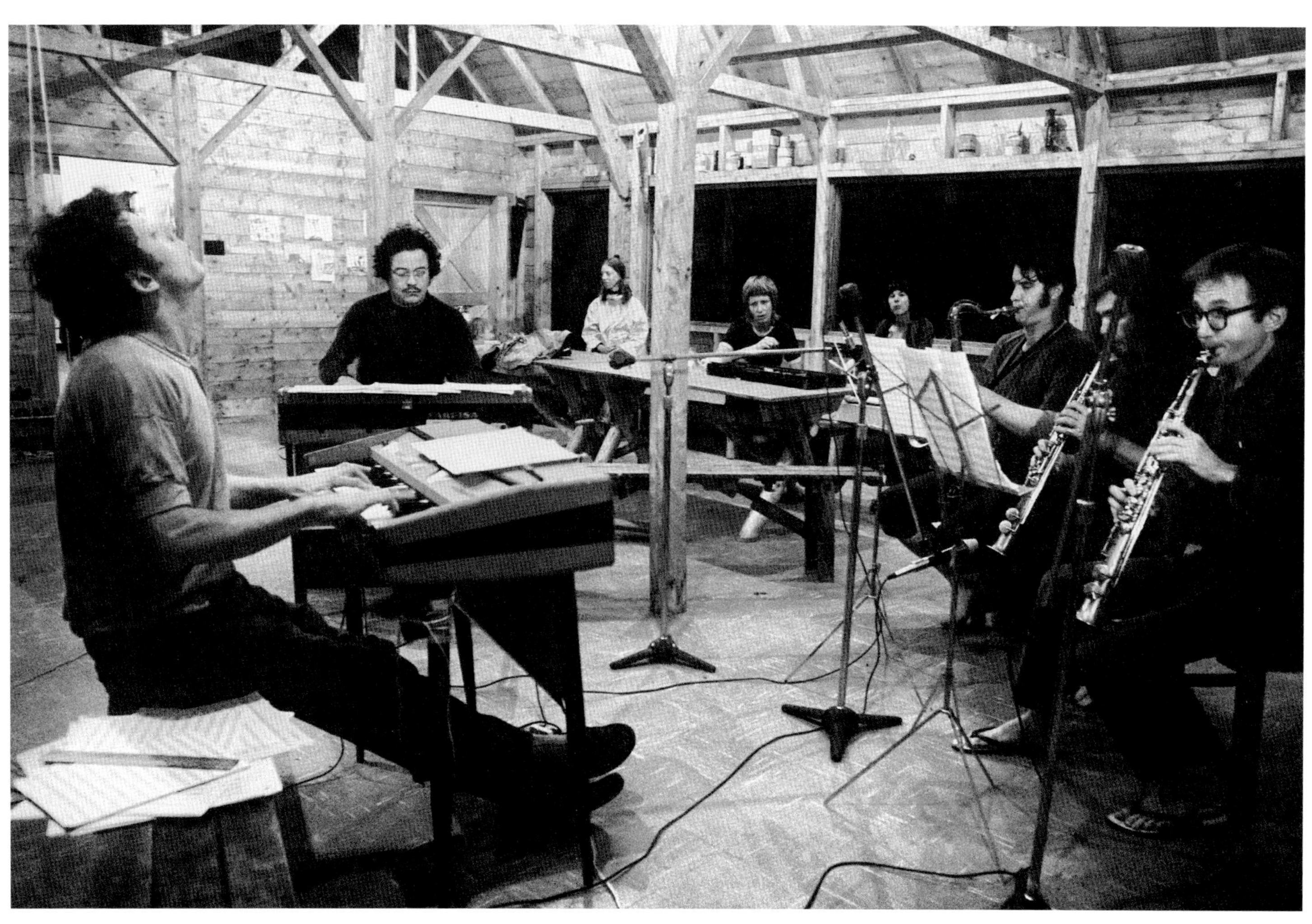

The ensemble pumps up the volume

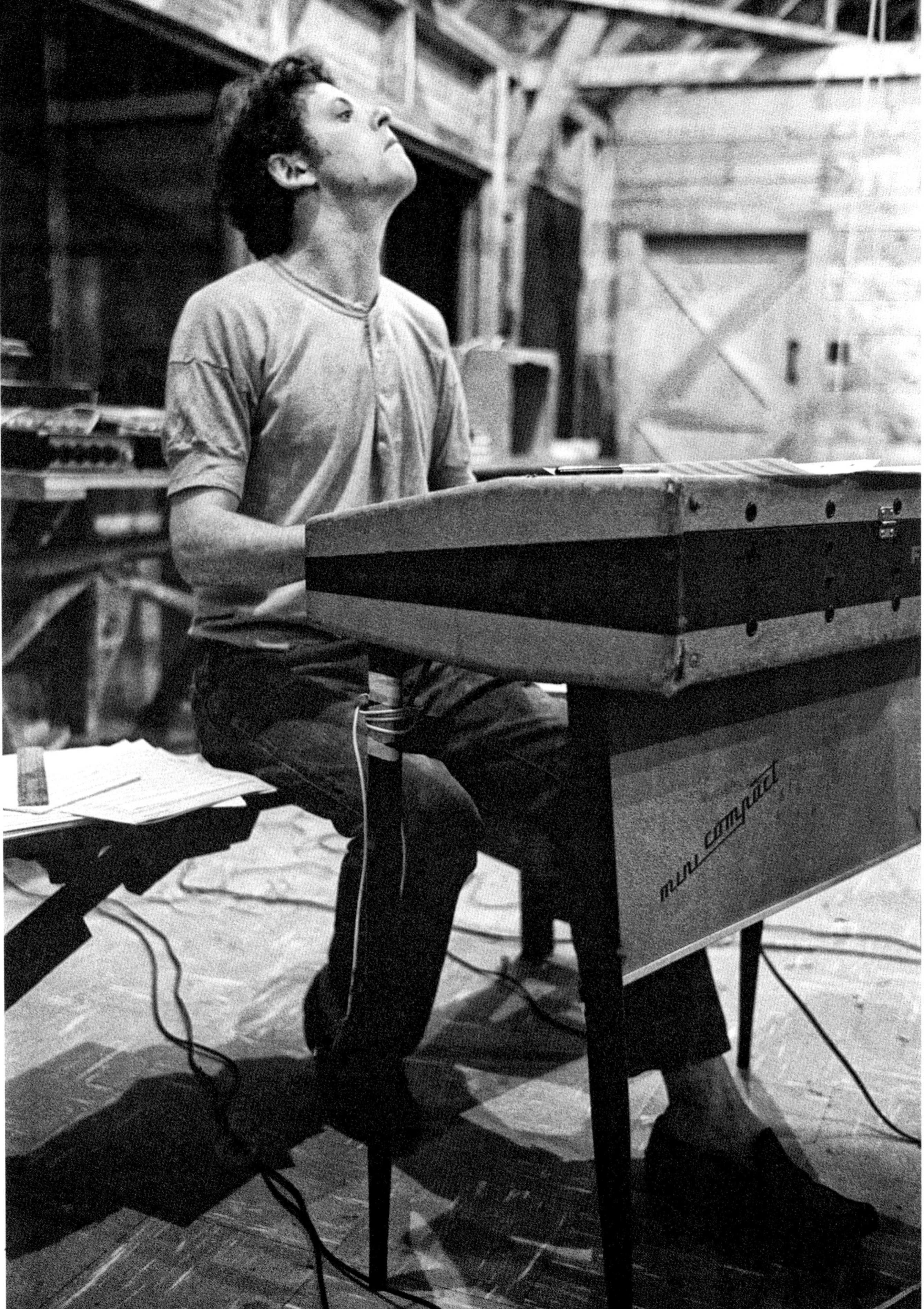
mini compact

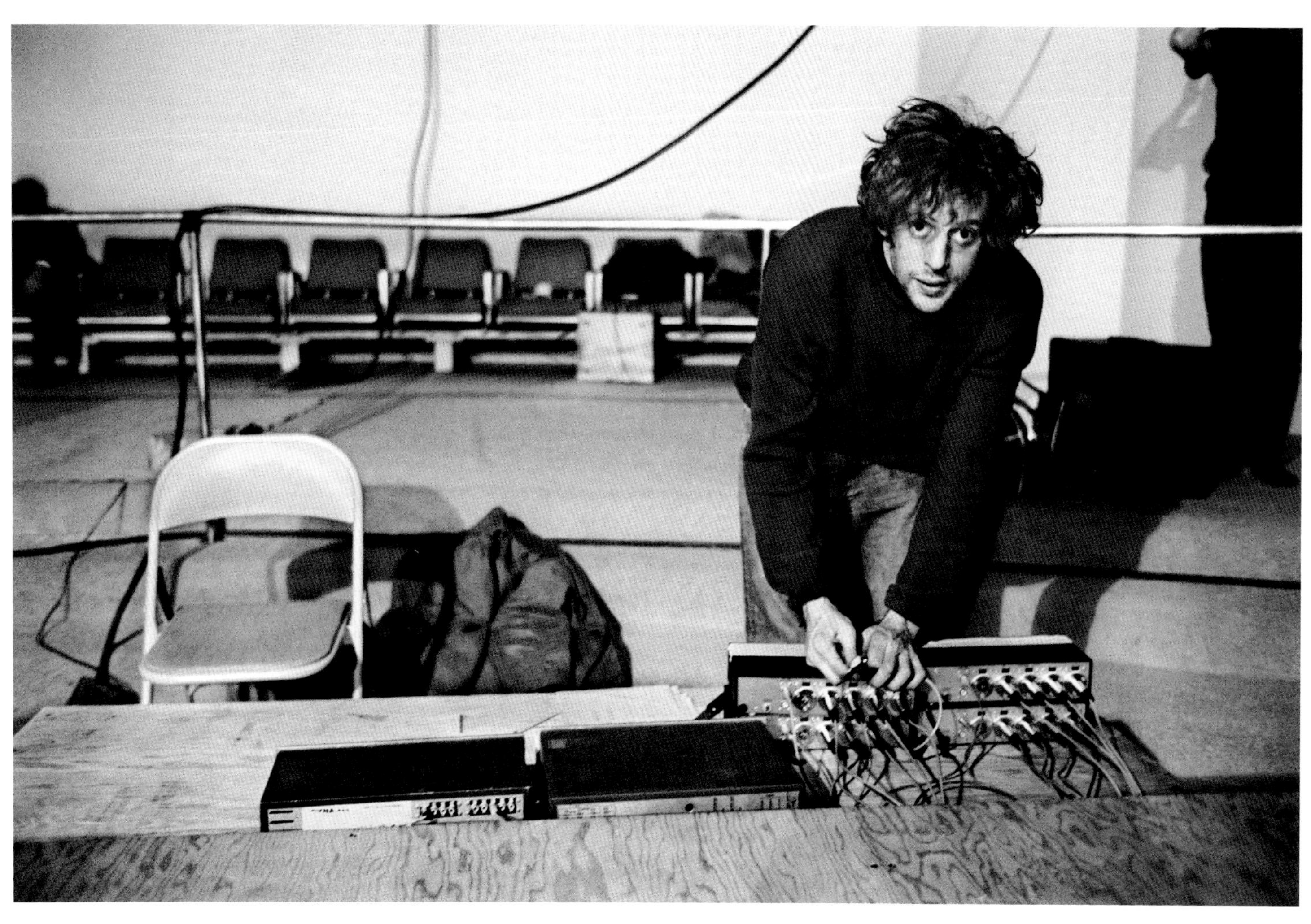

above, Philip doing sound check for Mabou Mines

left, Philip in mid-flight

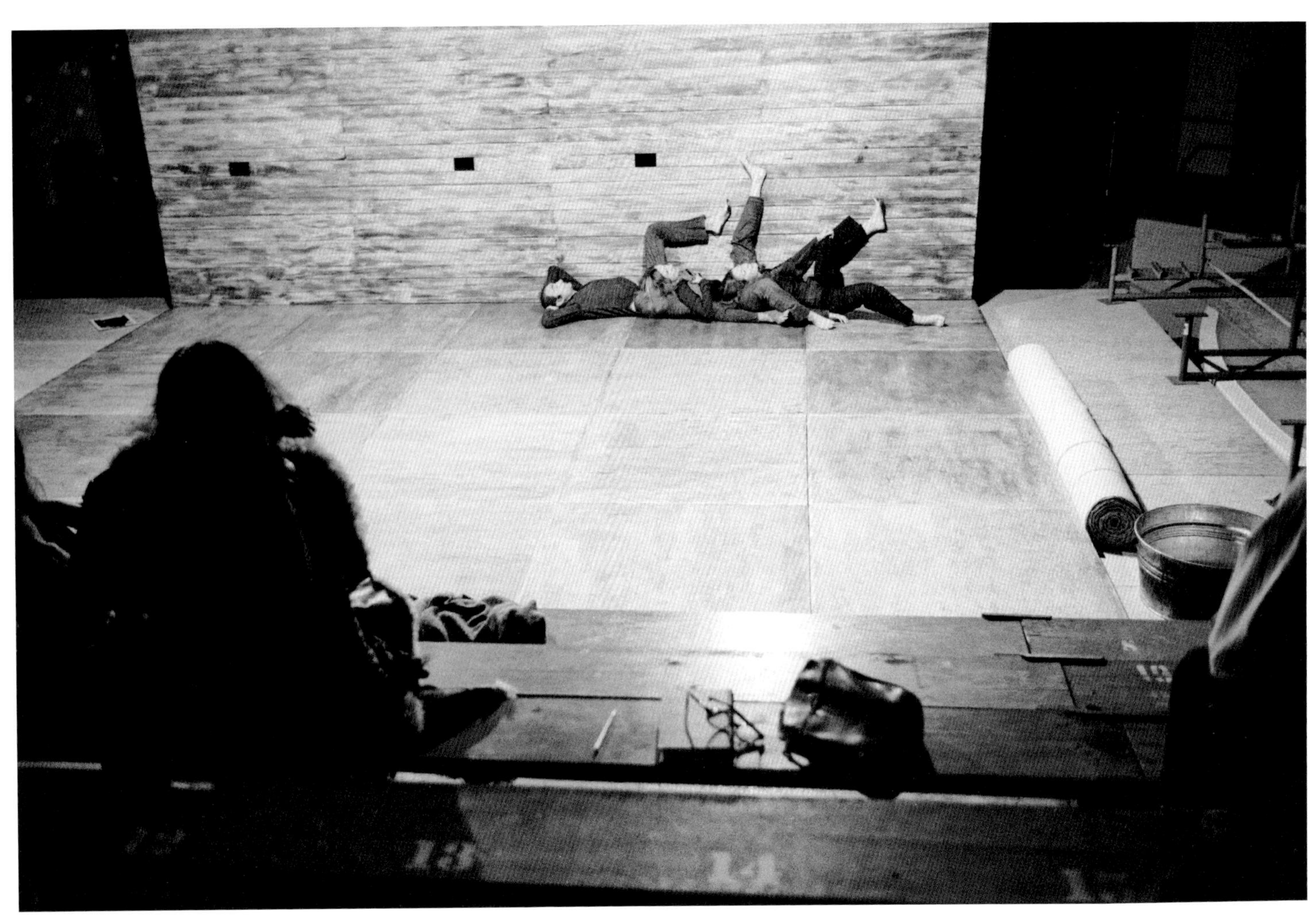

Mabou Mines group rehearsal

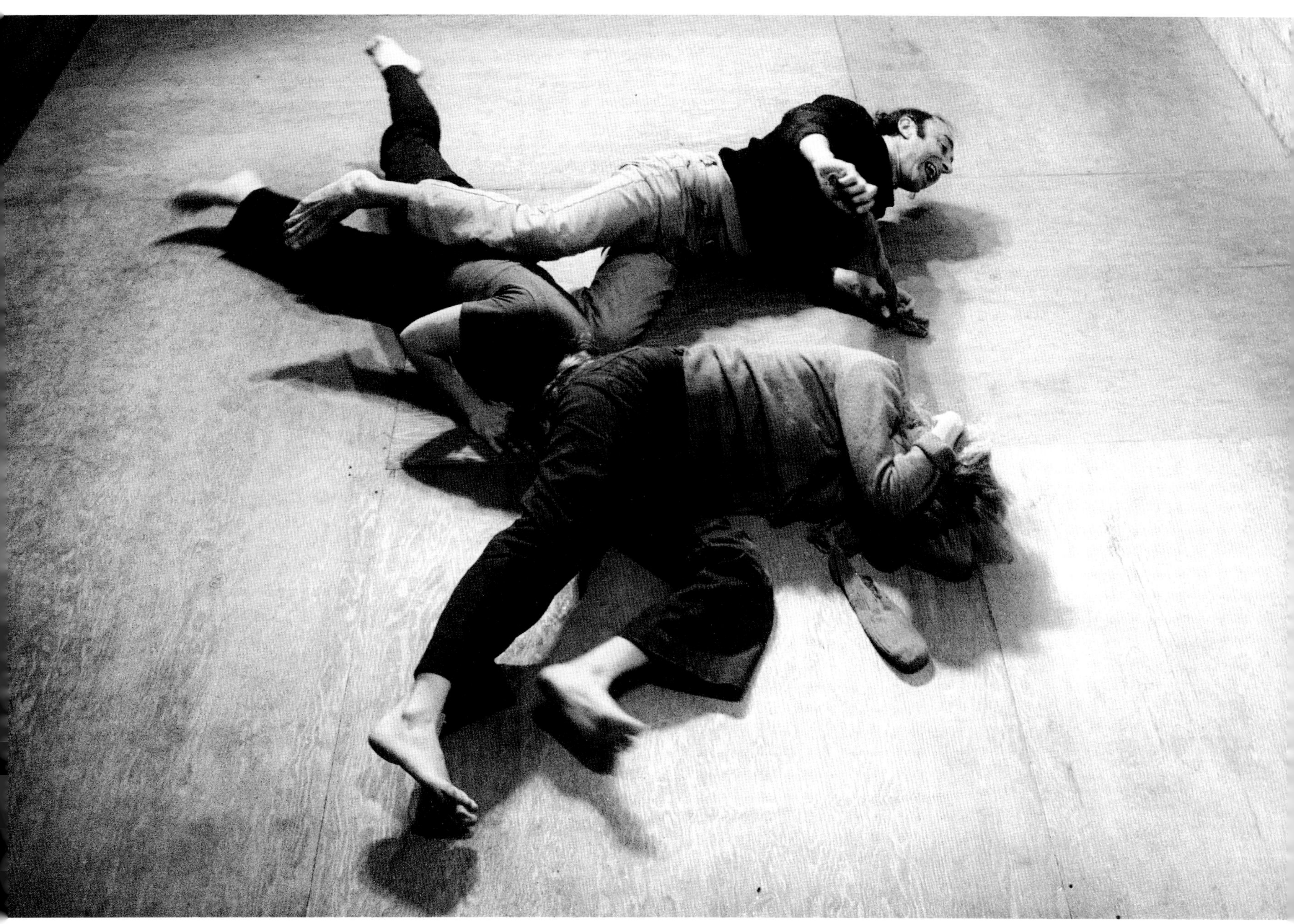

My memory of the first morning in Dunvegan waking up in a field by The Big House and seeing the intense colors of the sea, deep blue, the dark green trees, the bright green of the field (someone from Inverness once said there were four shades of green)—it was immediately inspiring—the colors would change continuously with the daily fluctuations of the weather/time/atmosphere—the sky seemed closer, the air so fresh and the wind—one is constantly aware of the wind as it whistles in the eaves, churns the sea, bends the trees, here we walk against the wind, we are blown around by the wind ... the sheer cliffs—some shale, some a harder granite-like rock and clay with a waterfall that was used as a shower on the beach—the rocks the stones all shades of grey black sand rust red, and coal mines extending under the sea. And from this and from other Islands came the music, the high piercing sounds of the fiddle, repeating melodies in a driving force that inspired movement in the landscape. All that became part of my work.

Joan Jonas

Joan mapping the territory

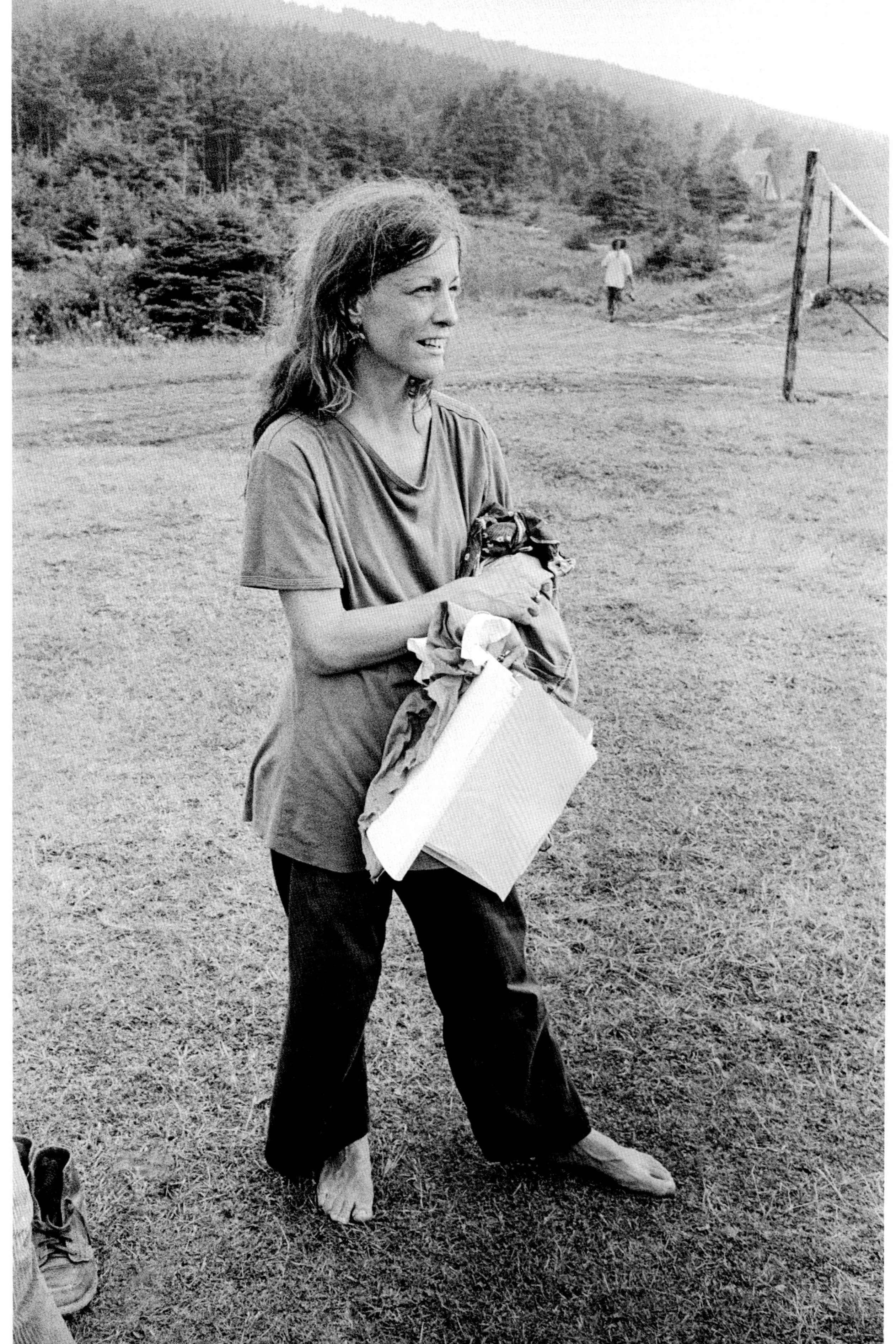

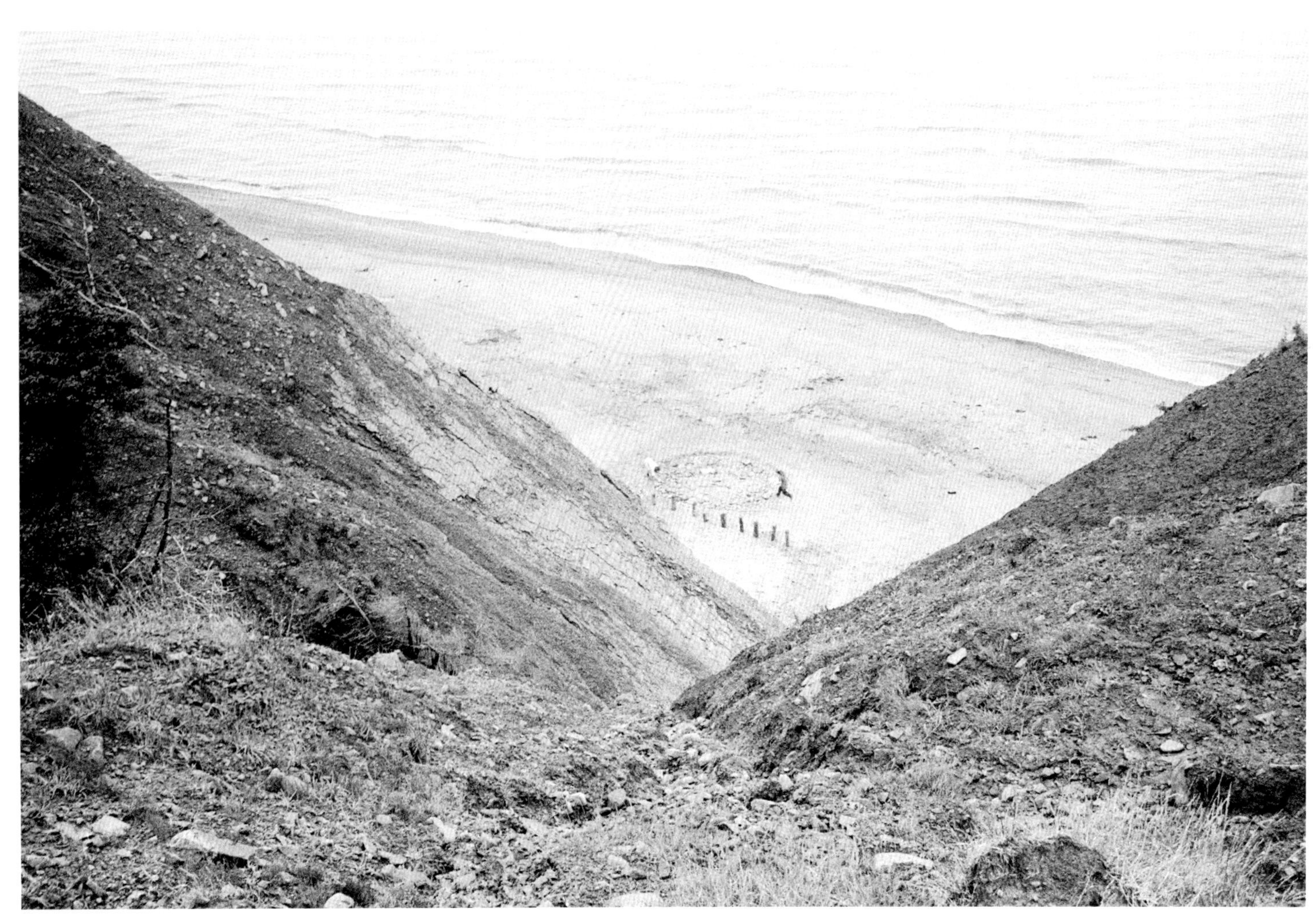

A Jonas beach performance piece

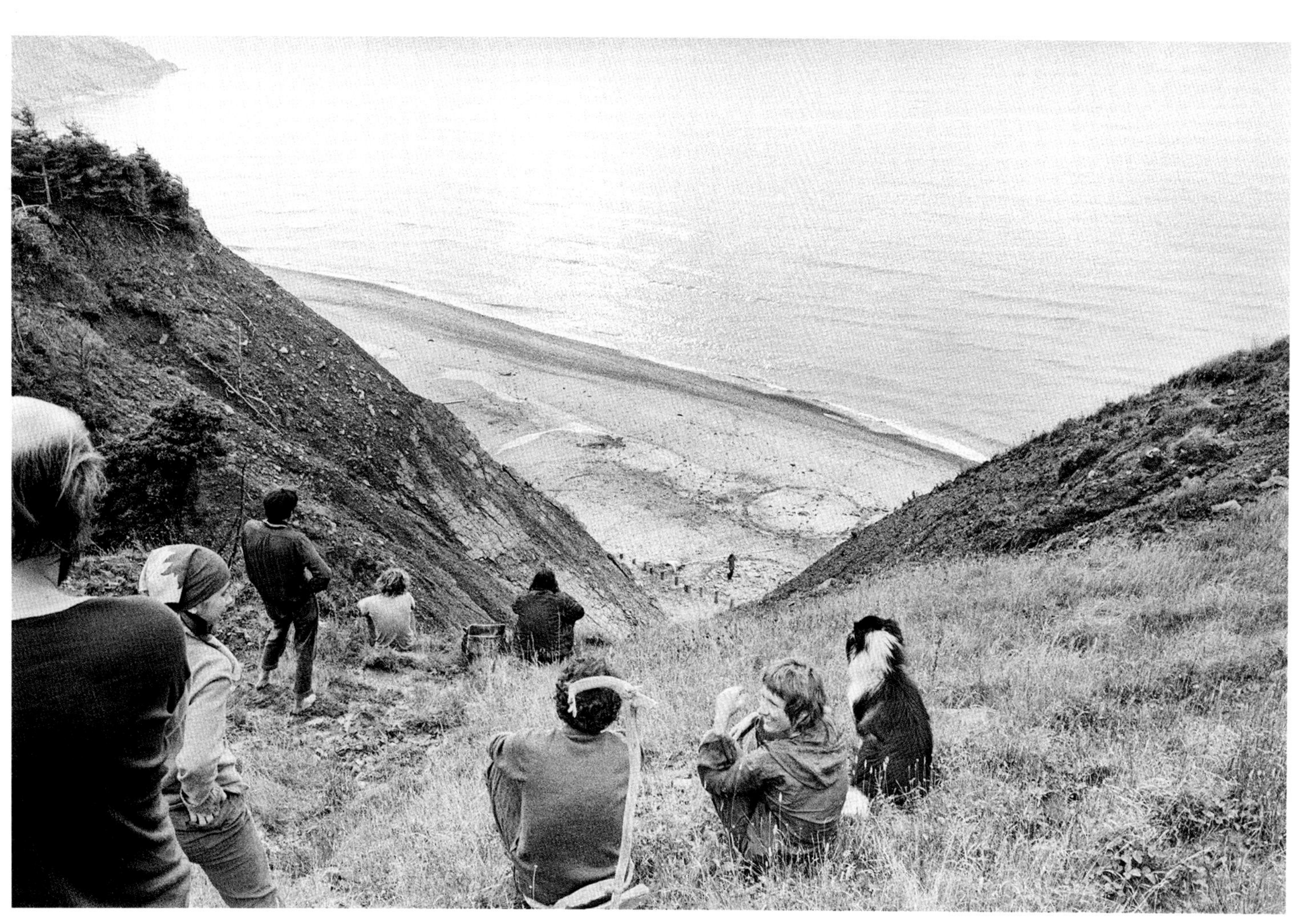

The audience assembles

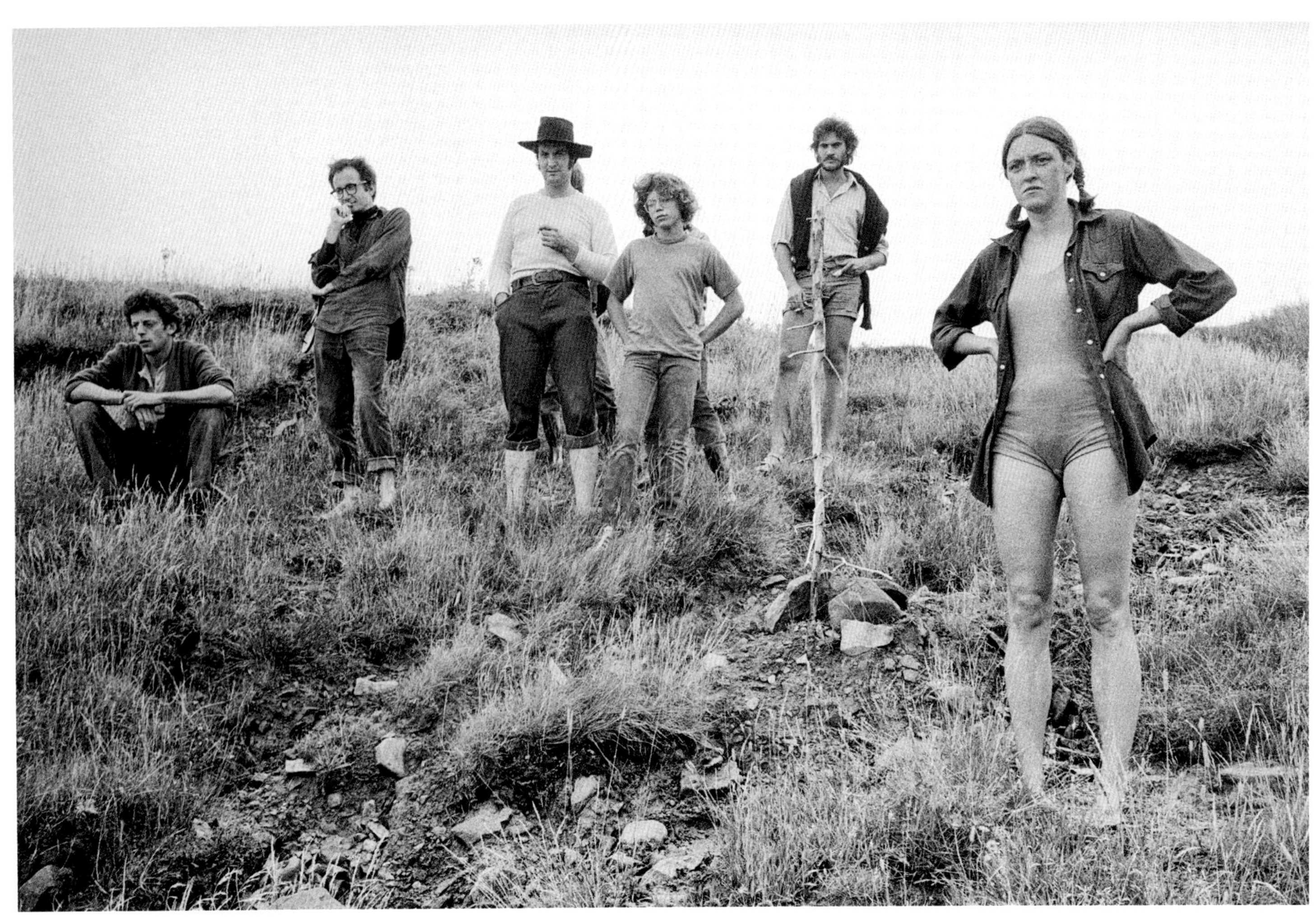

View from the balcony

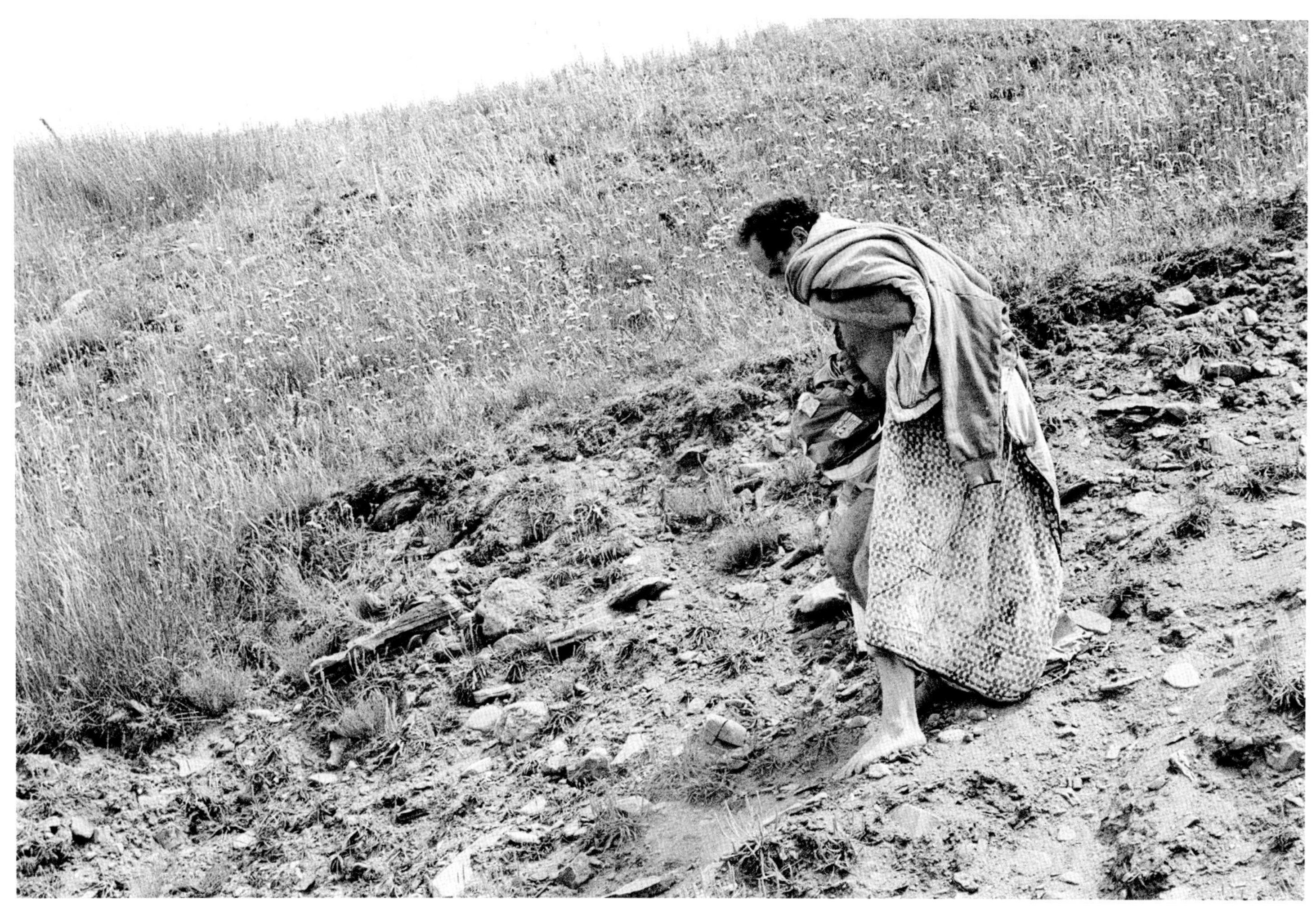

Robert descending to the beach

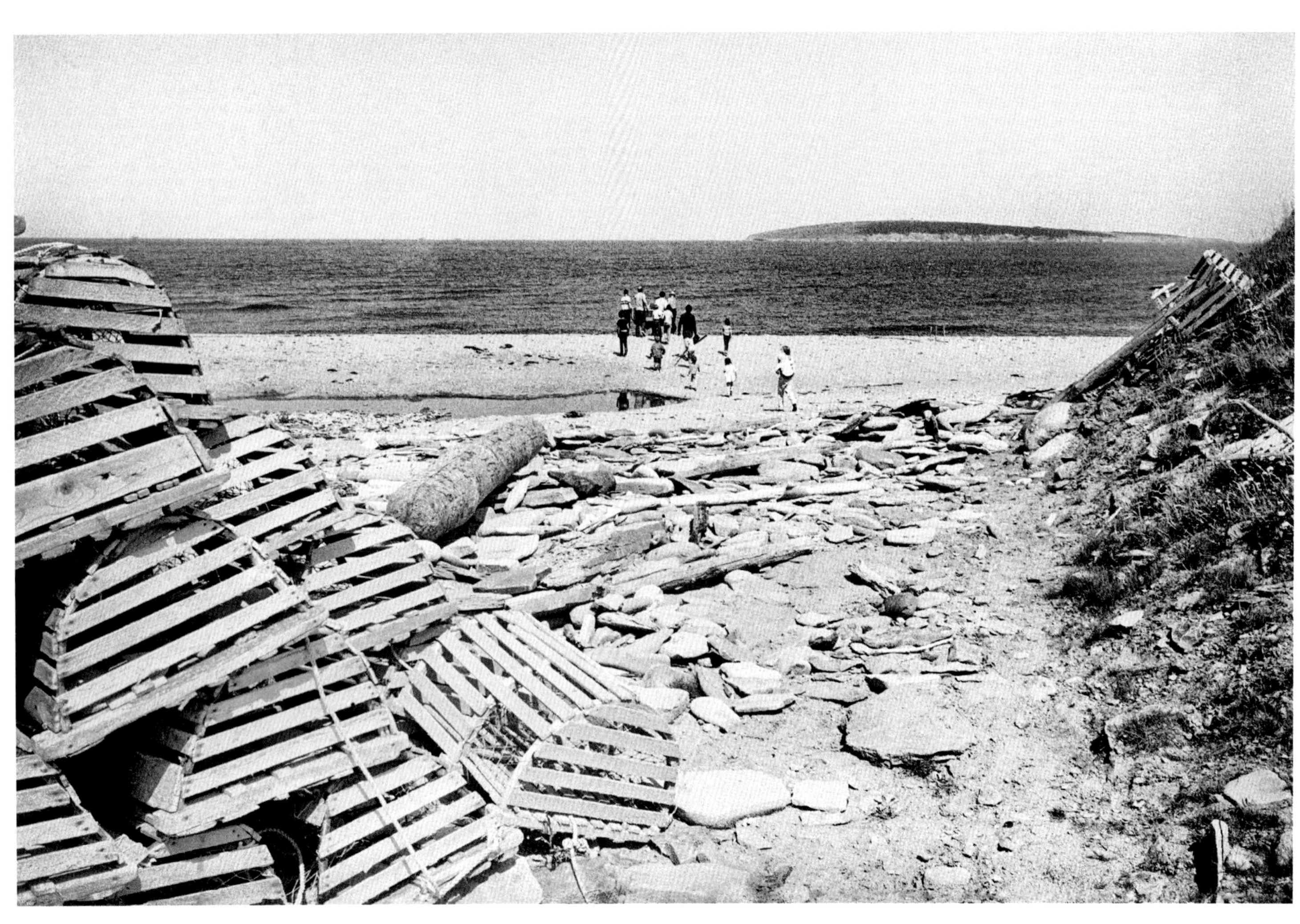

above, Contemplating a trip to Margaree

right, Portage to the water

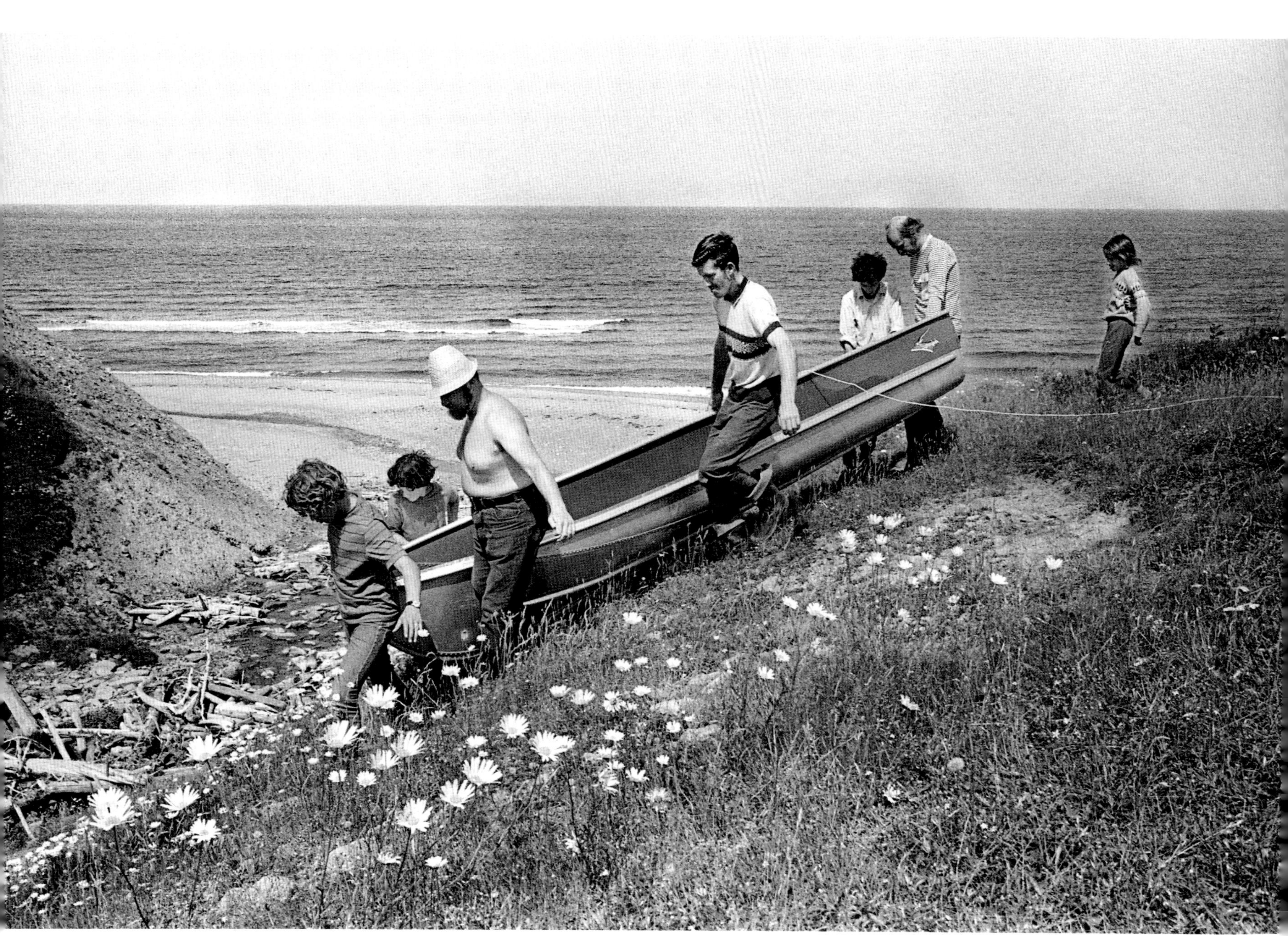

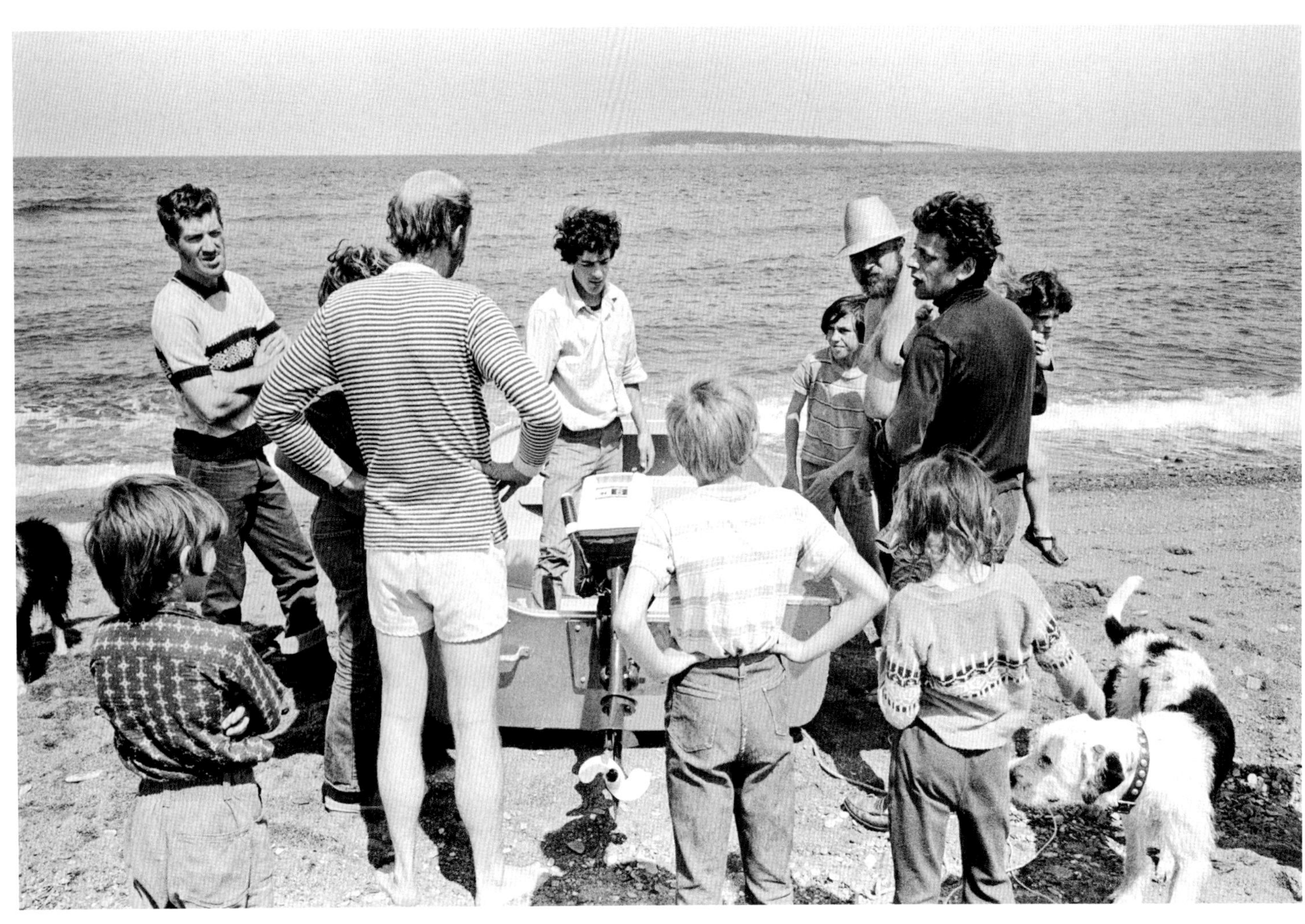

Voyage to the Island

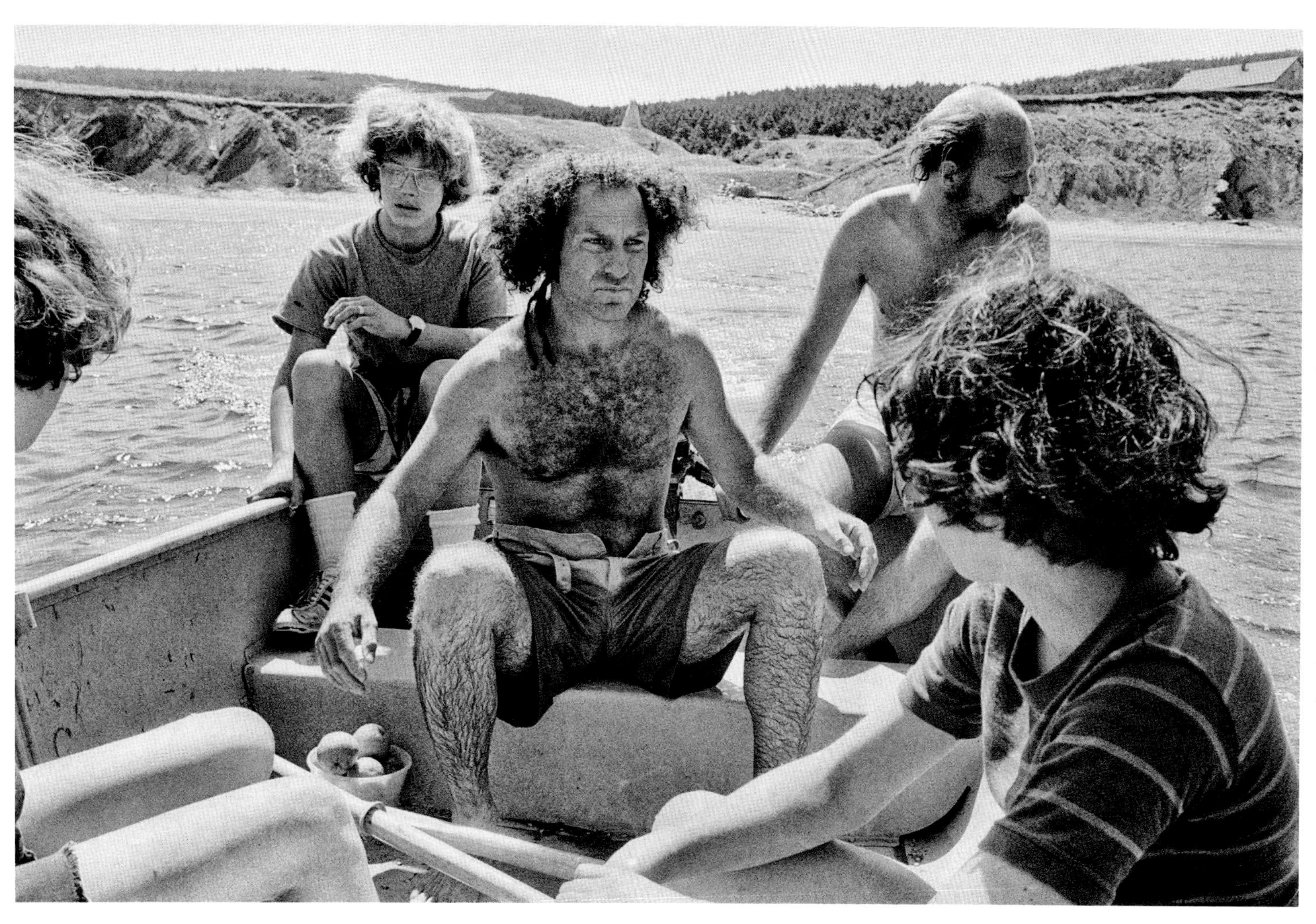

Greg, Rudy, the Katz kids, and The Captain

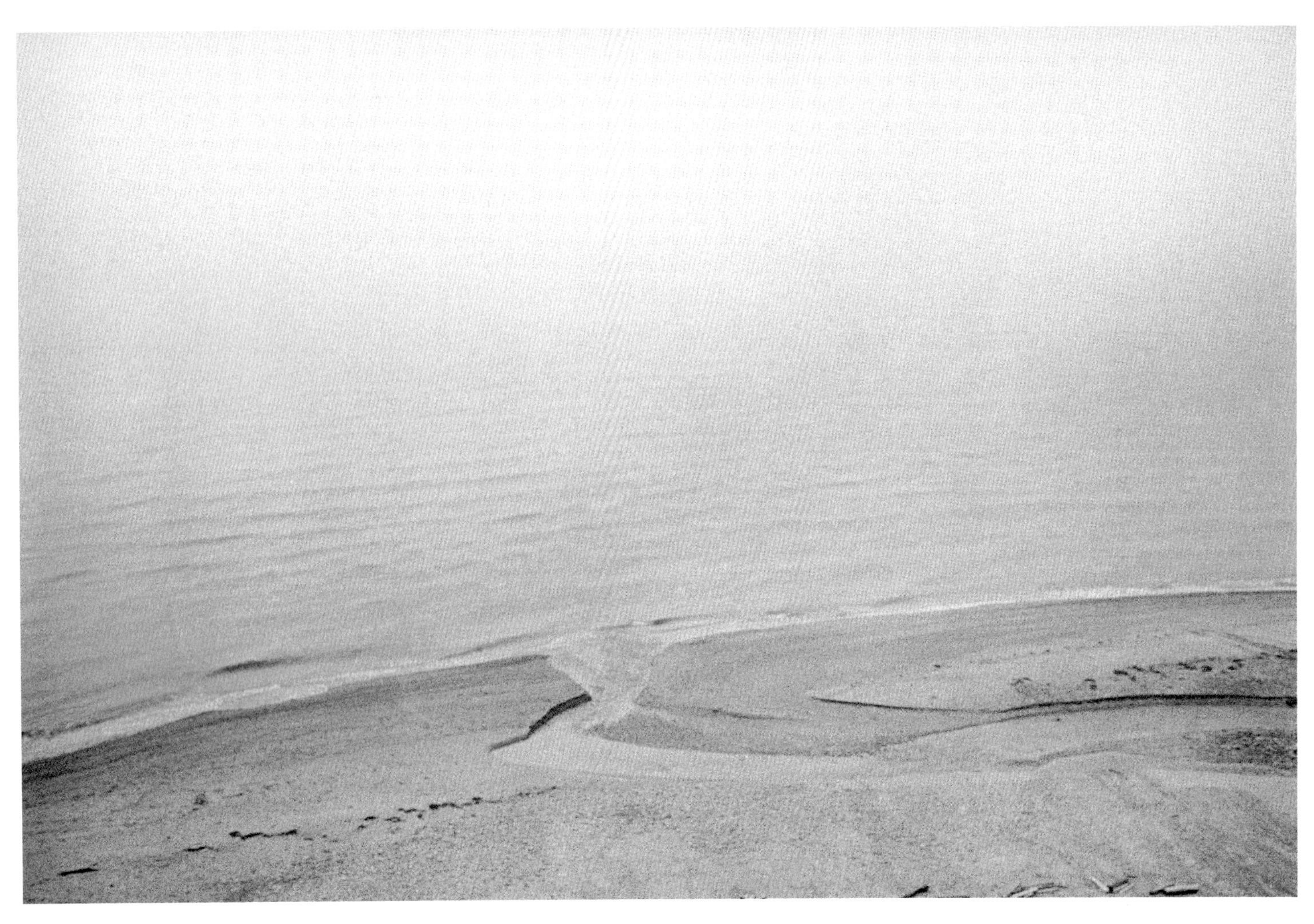

above, Faraway, so close

right, Greg on whale watch

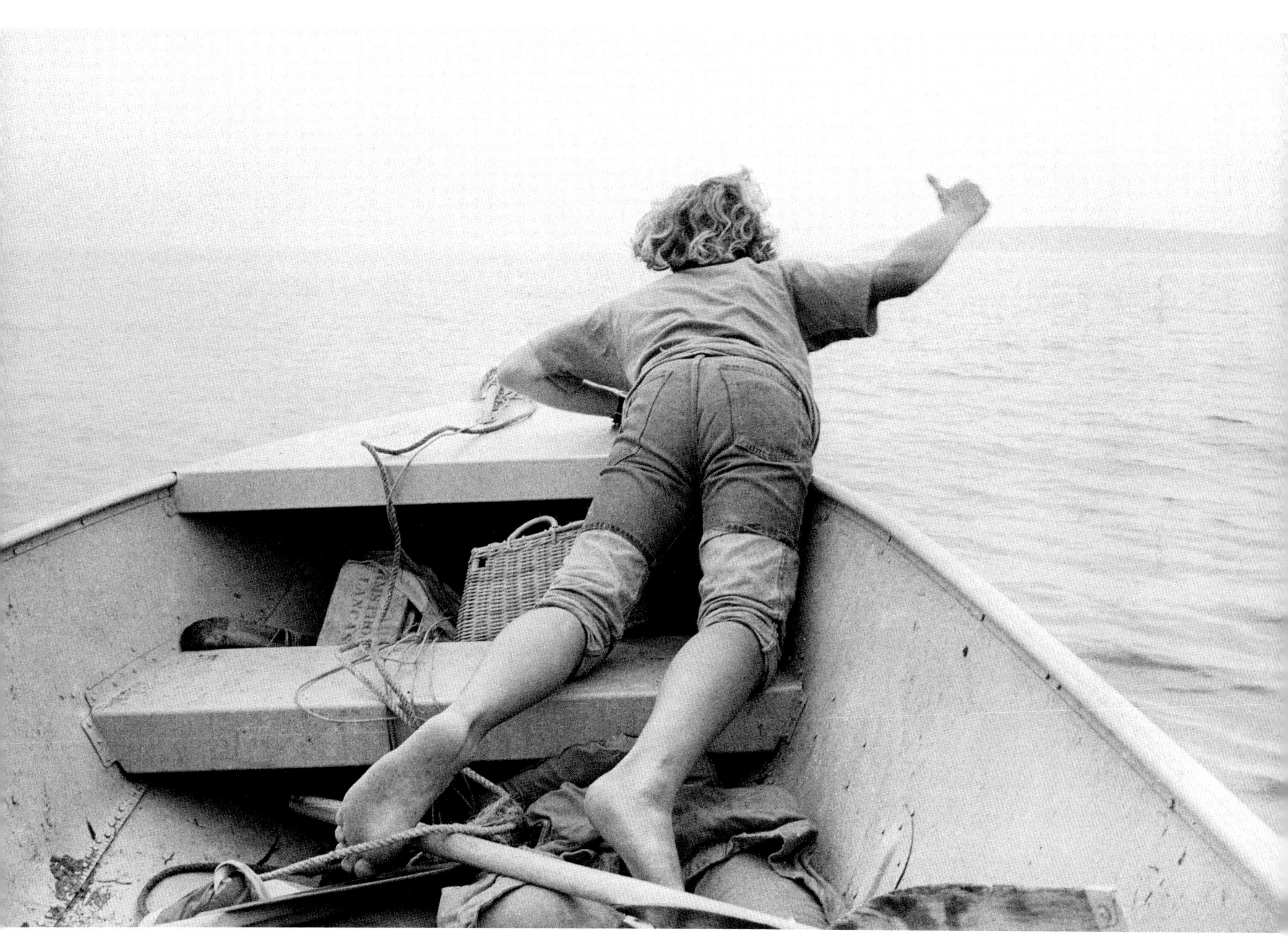

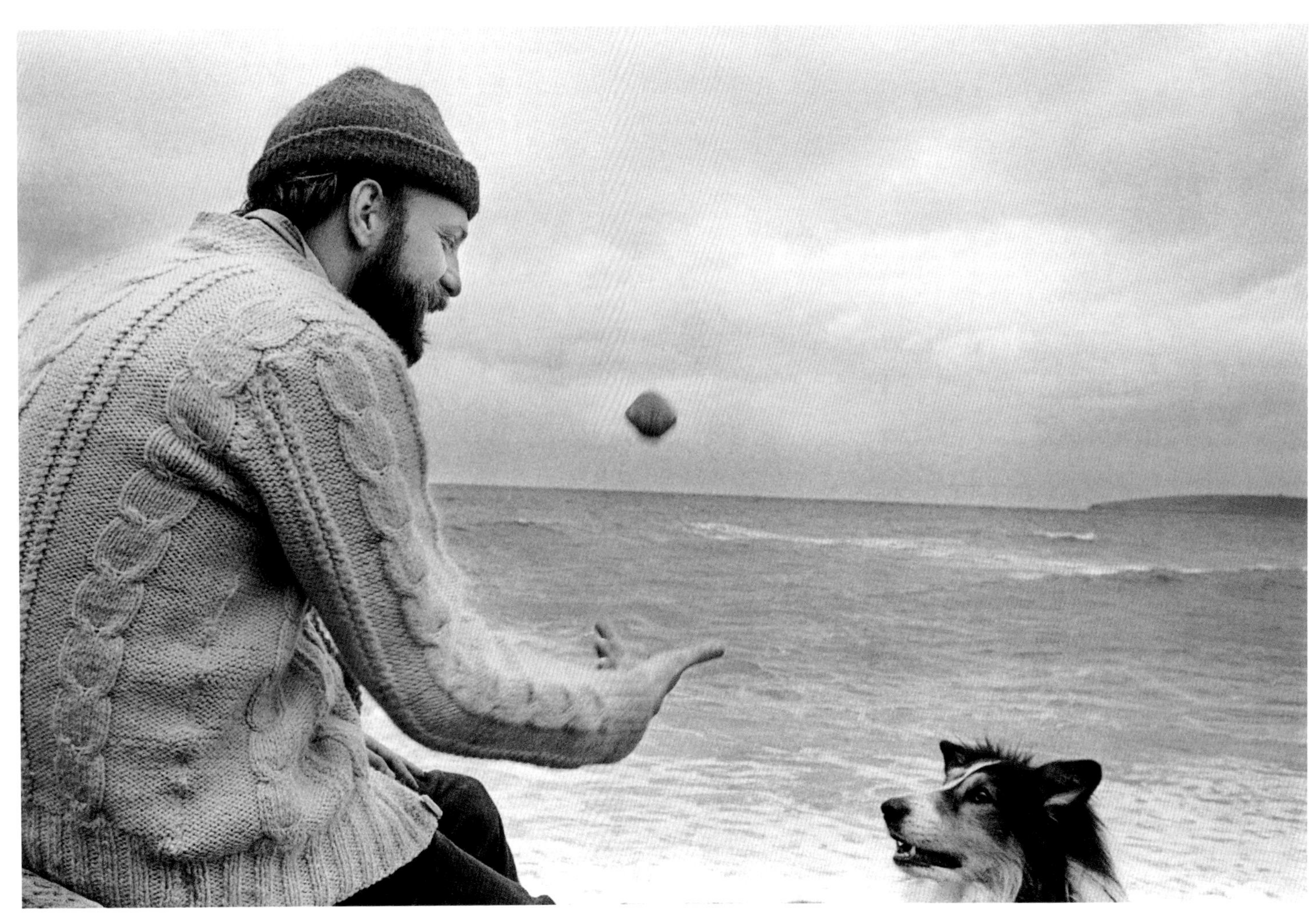

Rudy with Joey

Margaree, long and low in the water

The past is just like everything else—it's a dream. And it's just as much of a fiction as if you were actually writing fiction and we choose to say or choose to remember or can't remember how to remember whatever it was you were trying to remember. It comes out filtered and redefined and has an envelope of fiction to it. Because we're all basically fiction.

Rudy Wurlitzer

Rudy, long distance information

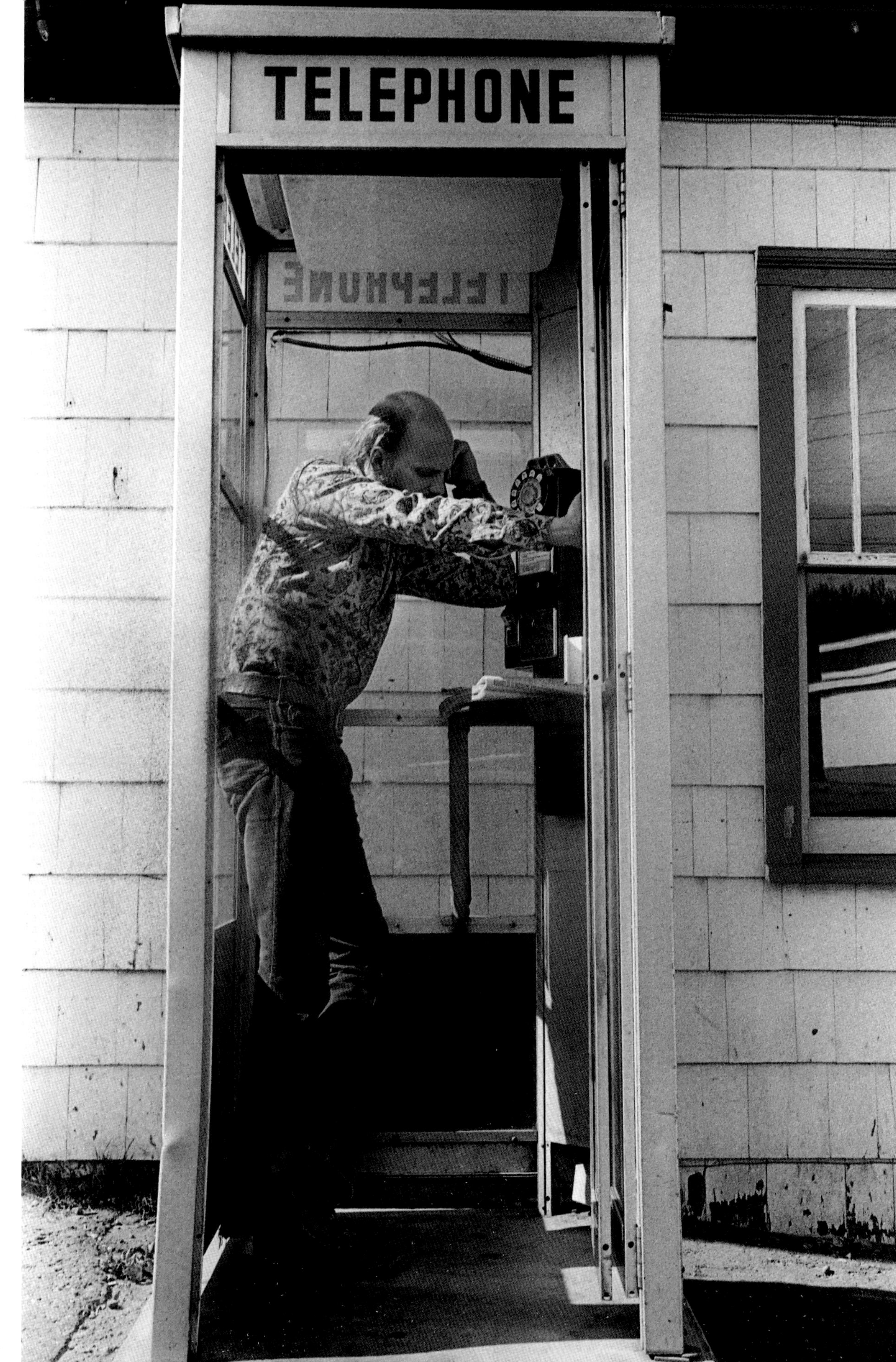
TELEPHONE

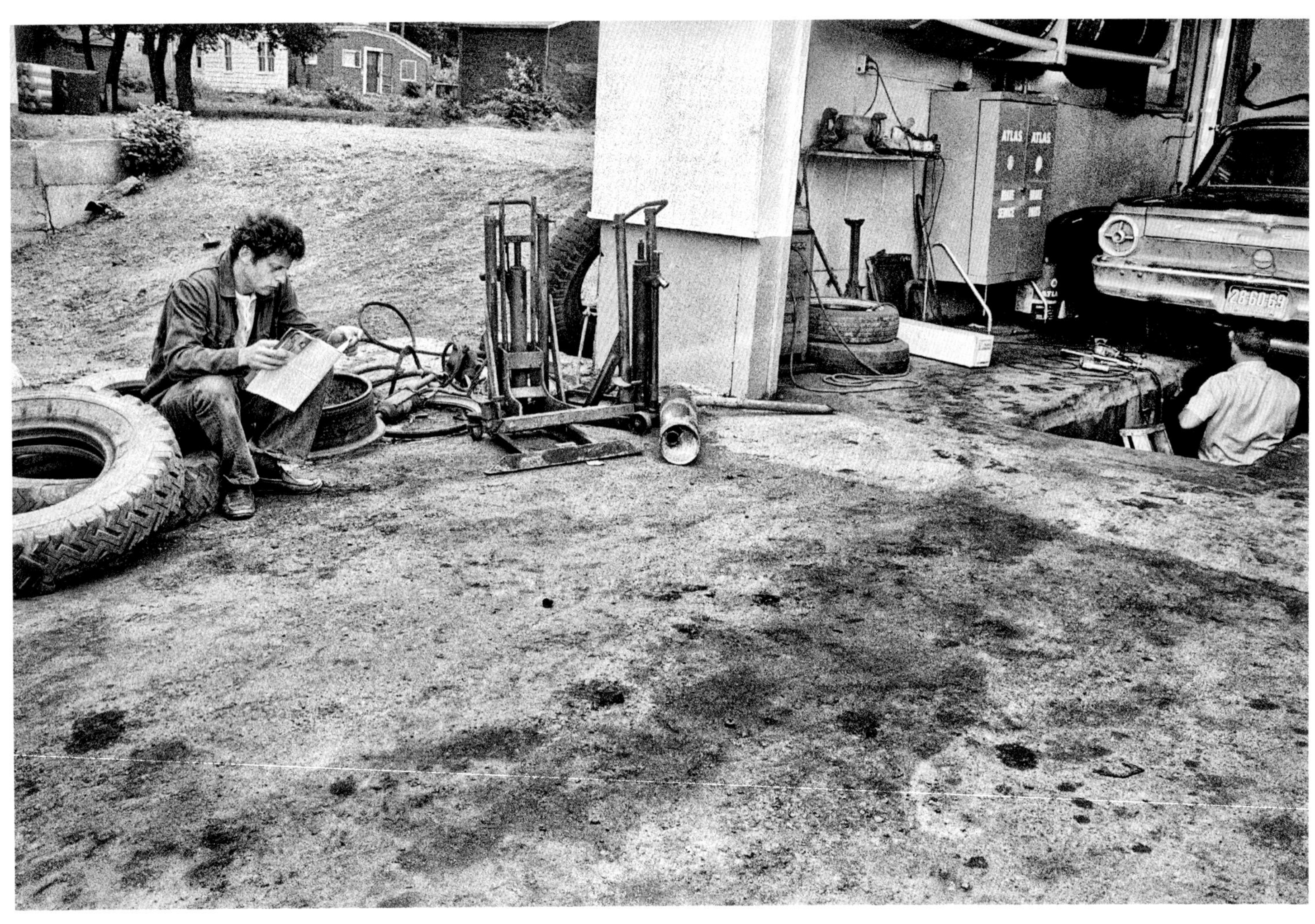

Philip gets the car fixed

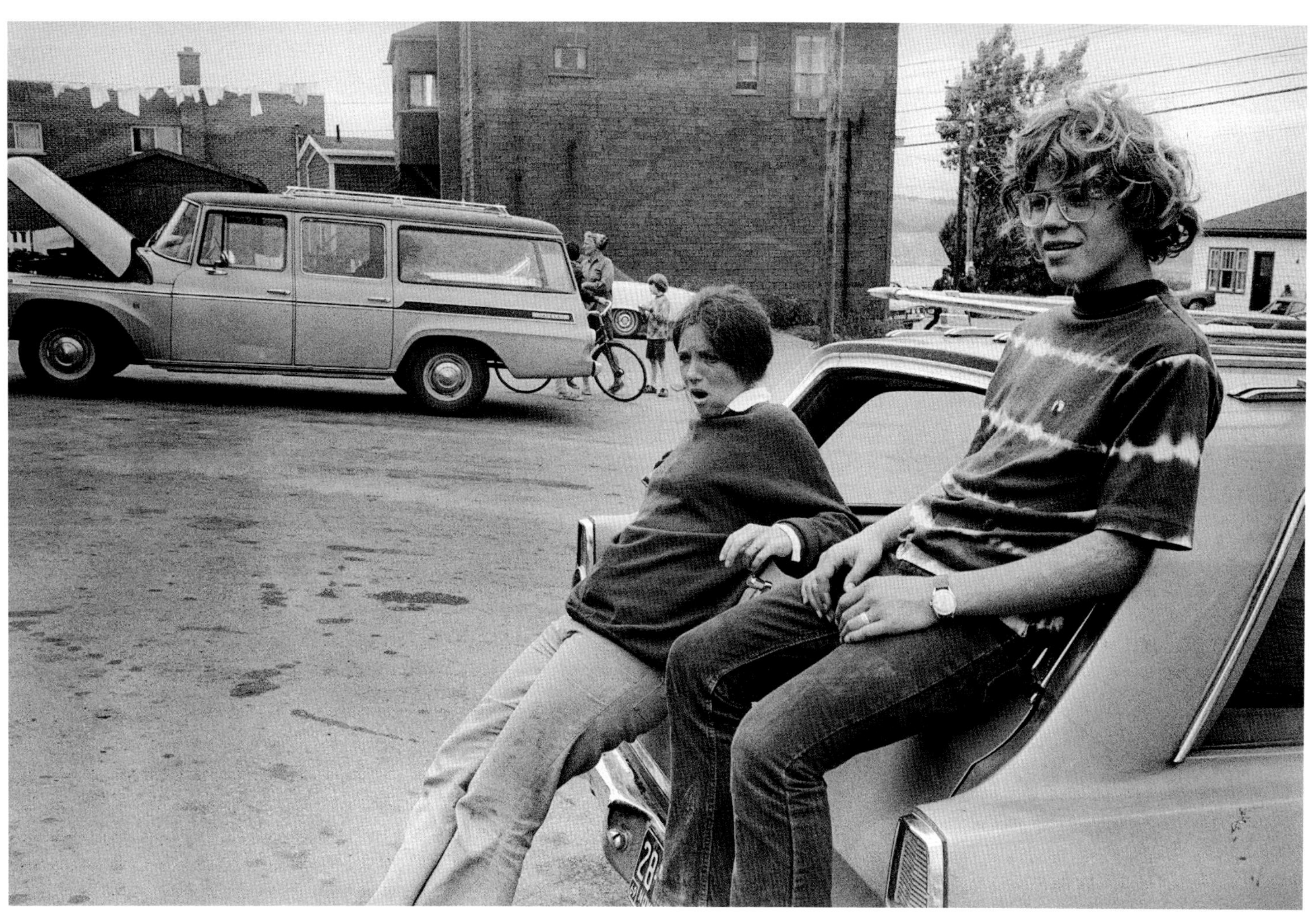

Greg and Helen with time on their hands

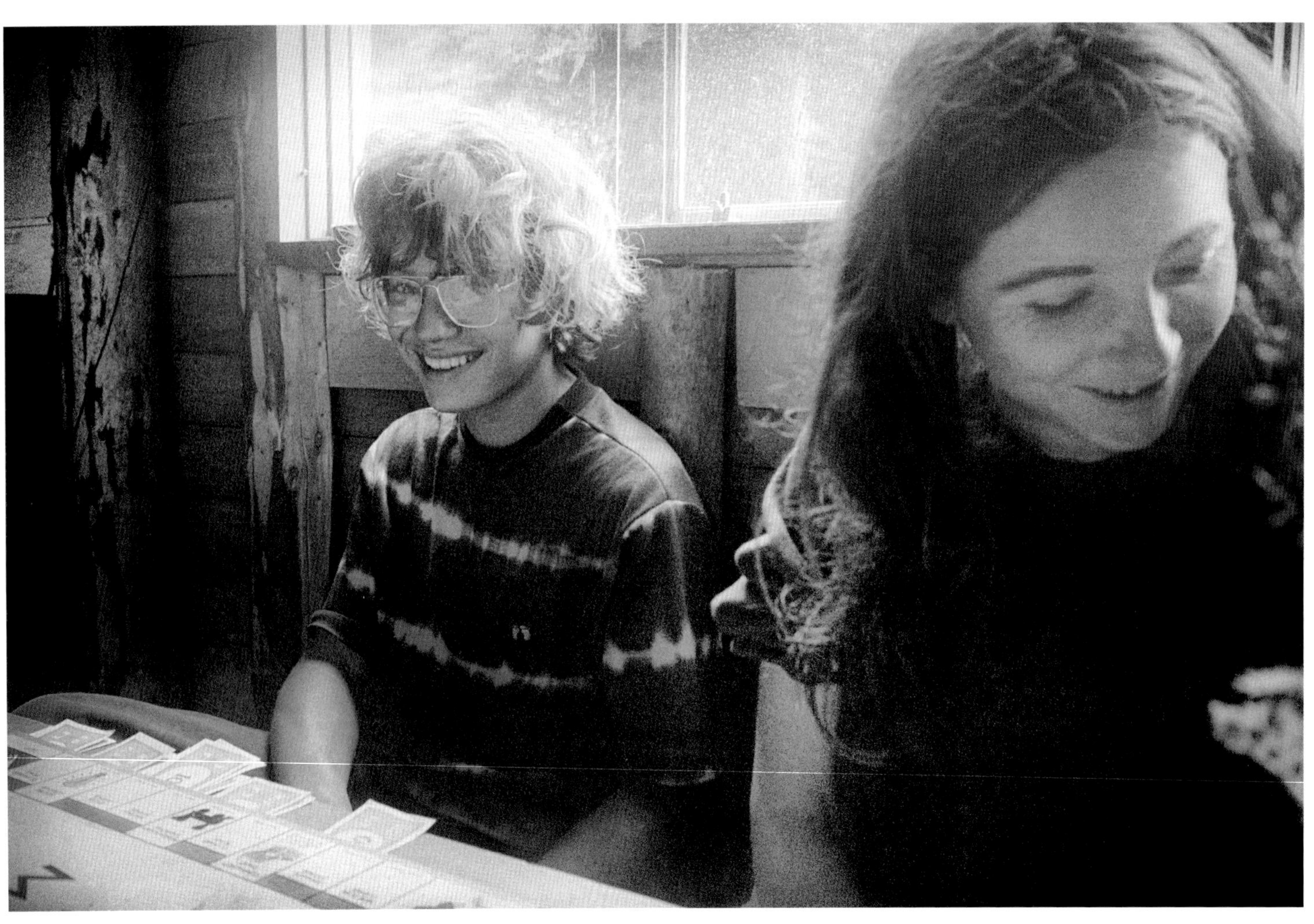

Greg triumphant over Helen at Monopoly

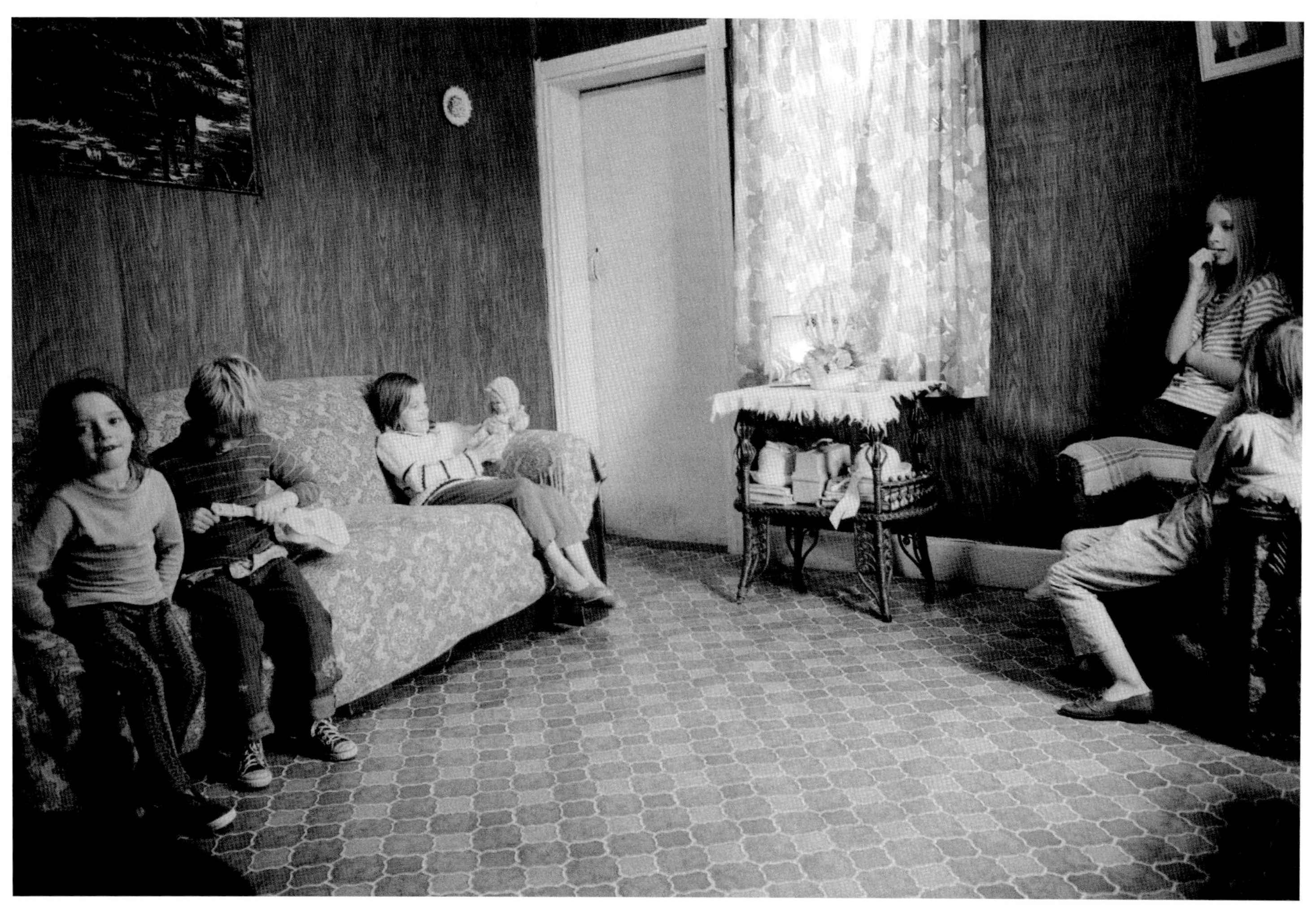

The MacPherson home

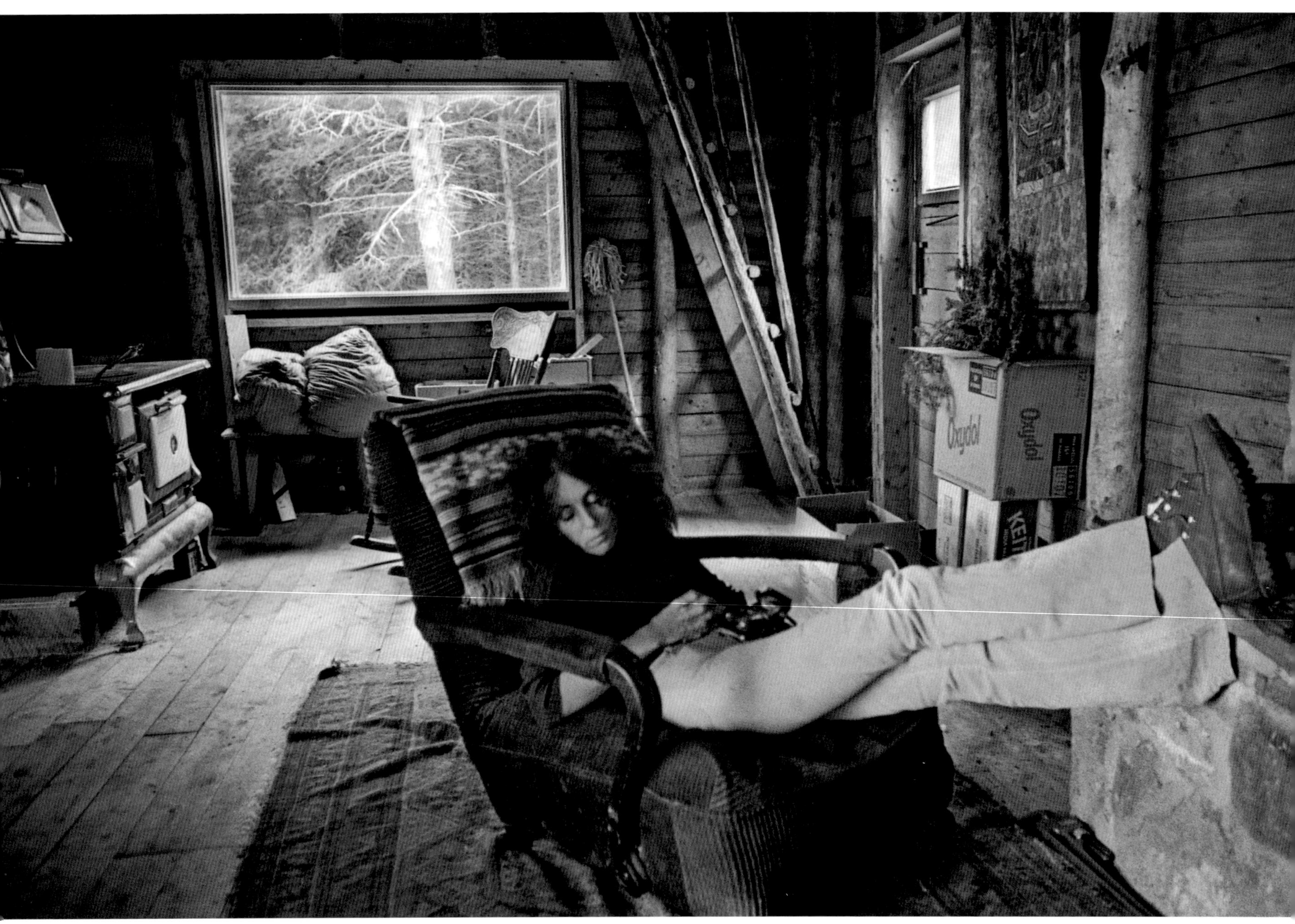
Oxydol
Oxydol

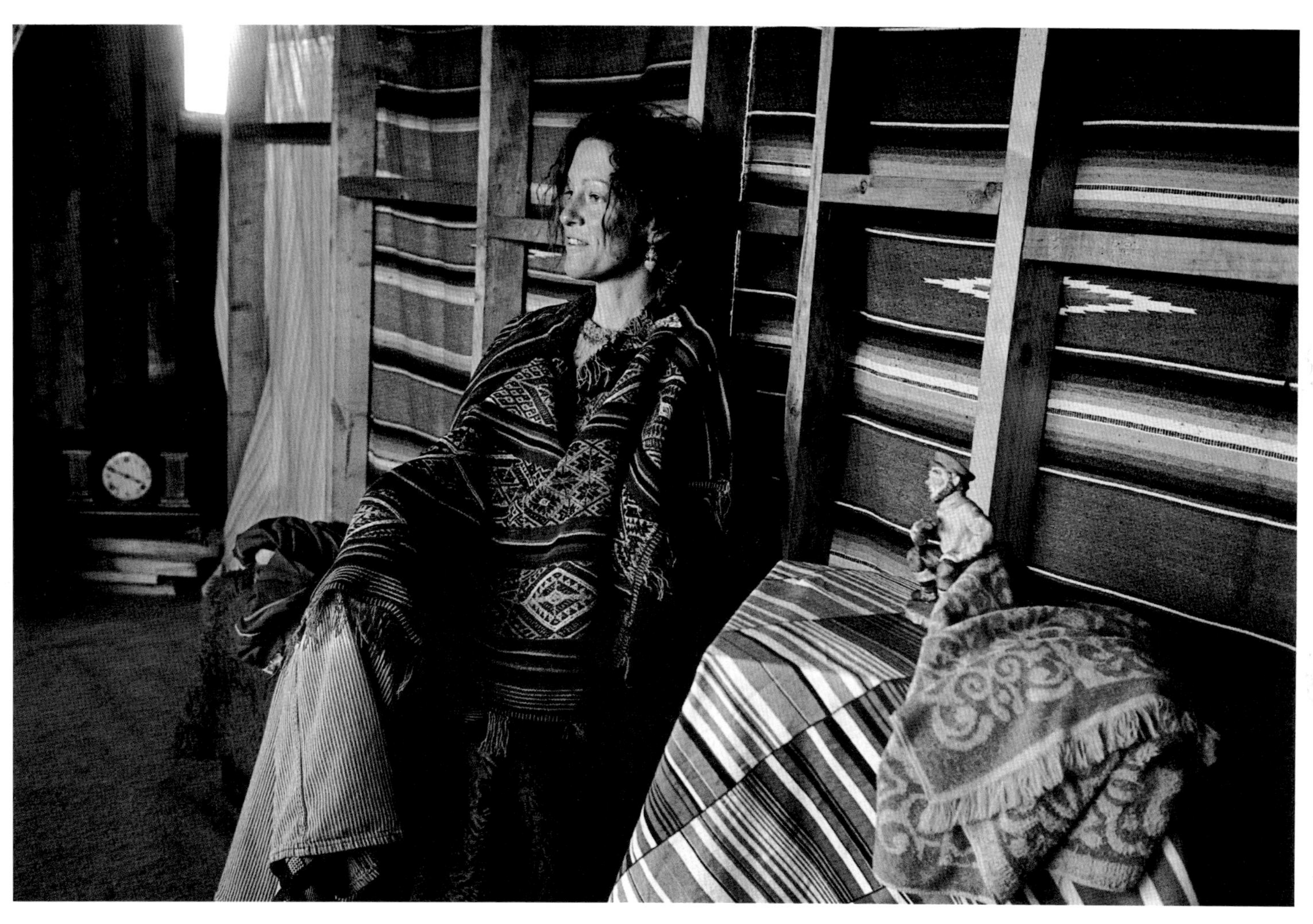

above, Joan in repose

left, Toby takes five

It was winter, and it was cold, and Robert knew I would do anything for him.

June Leaf

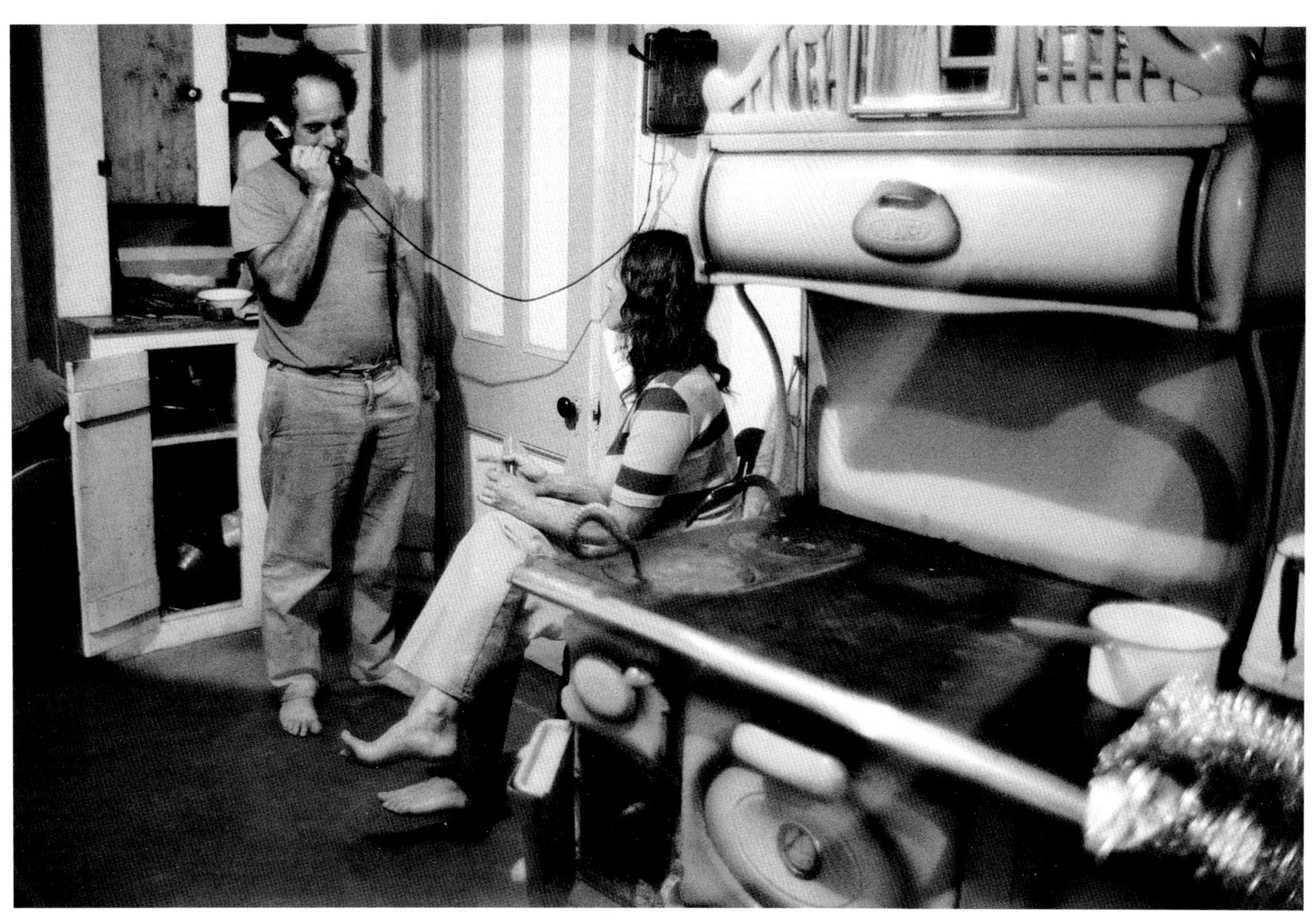

Domestic interior, Robert and June

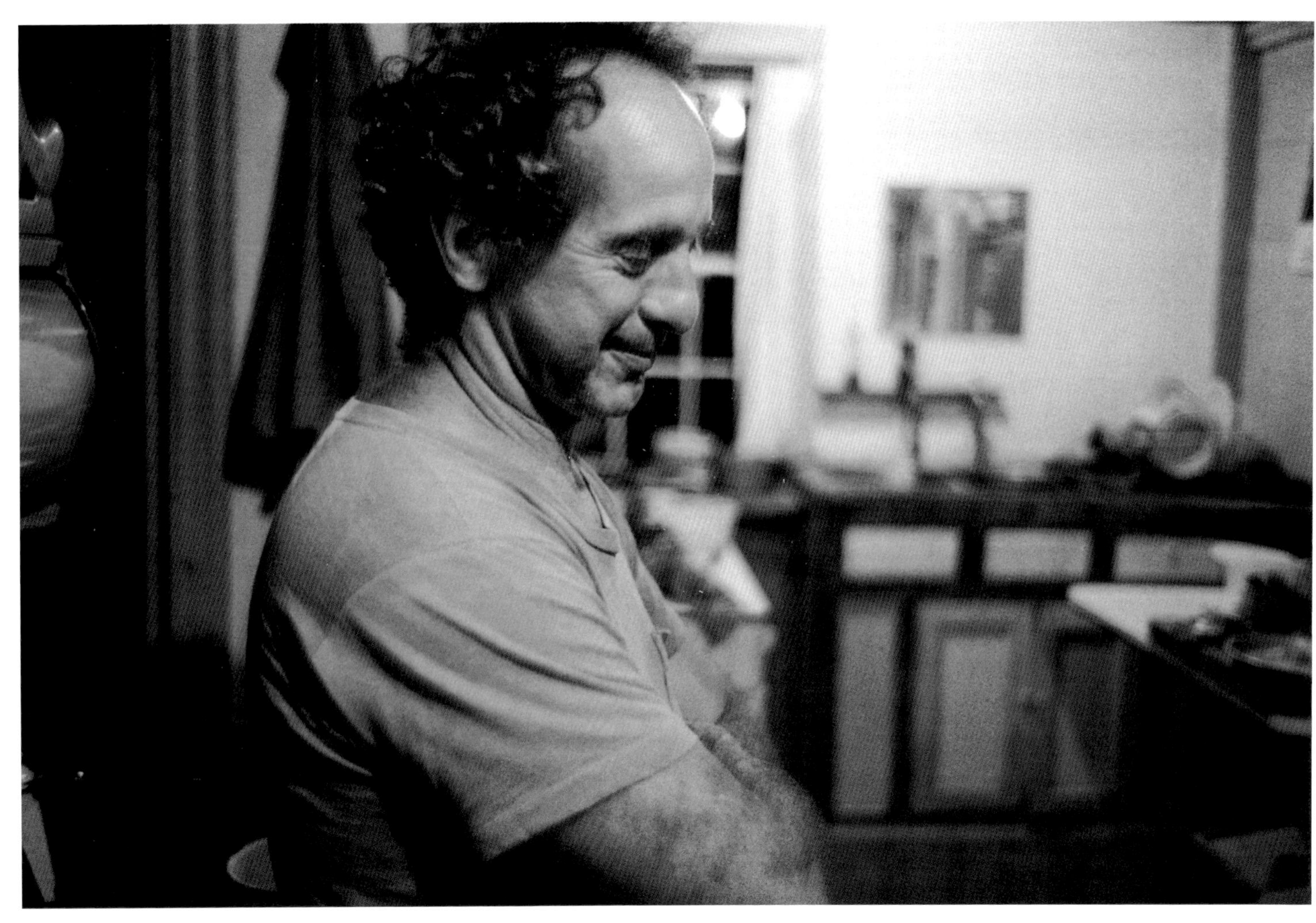

Robert gets the joke

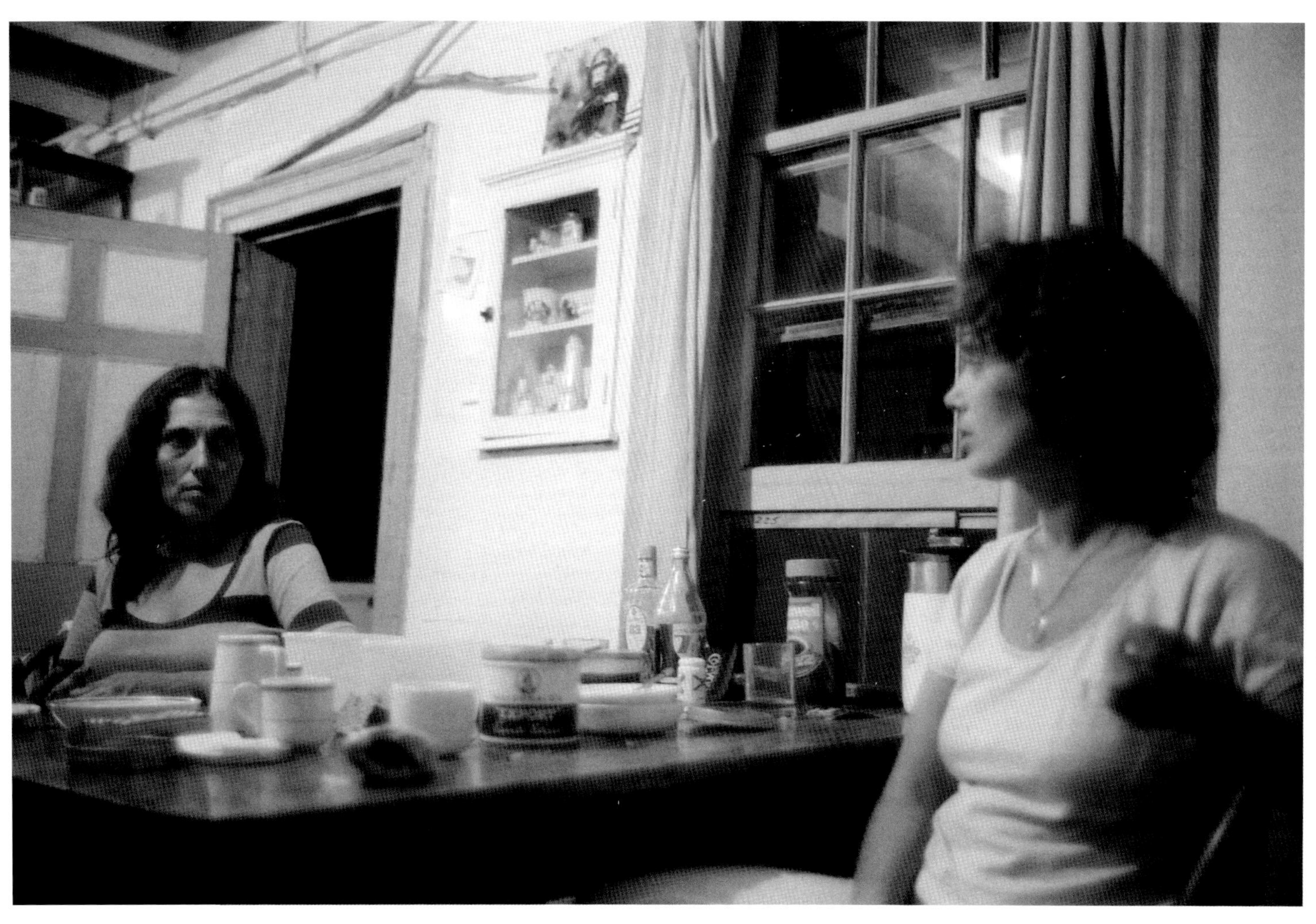

June and Roberta

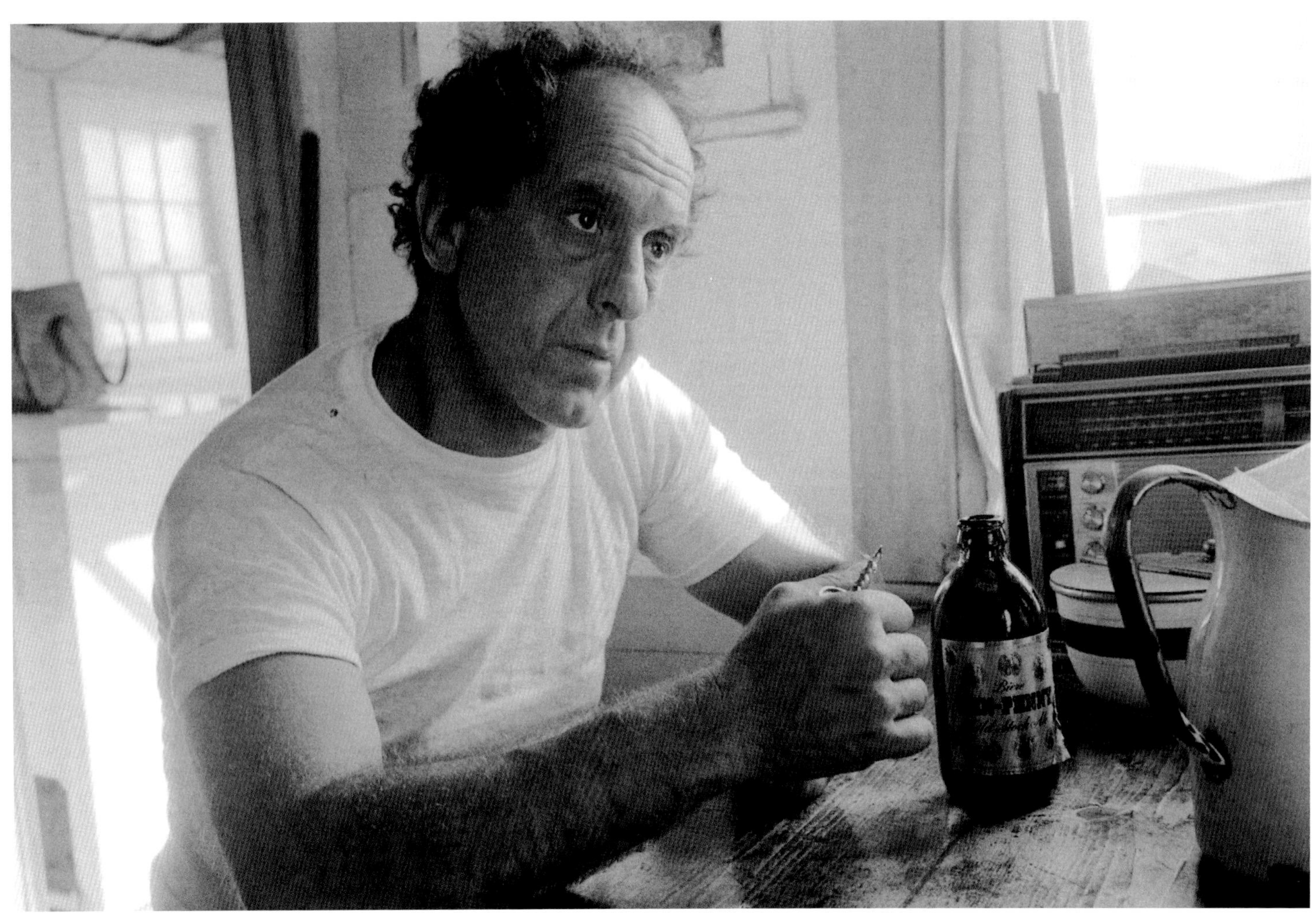

Robert

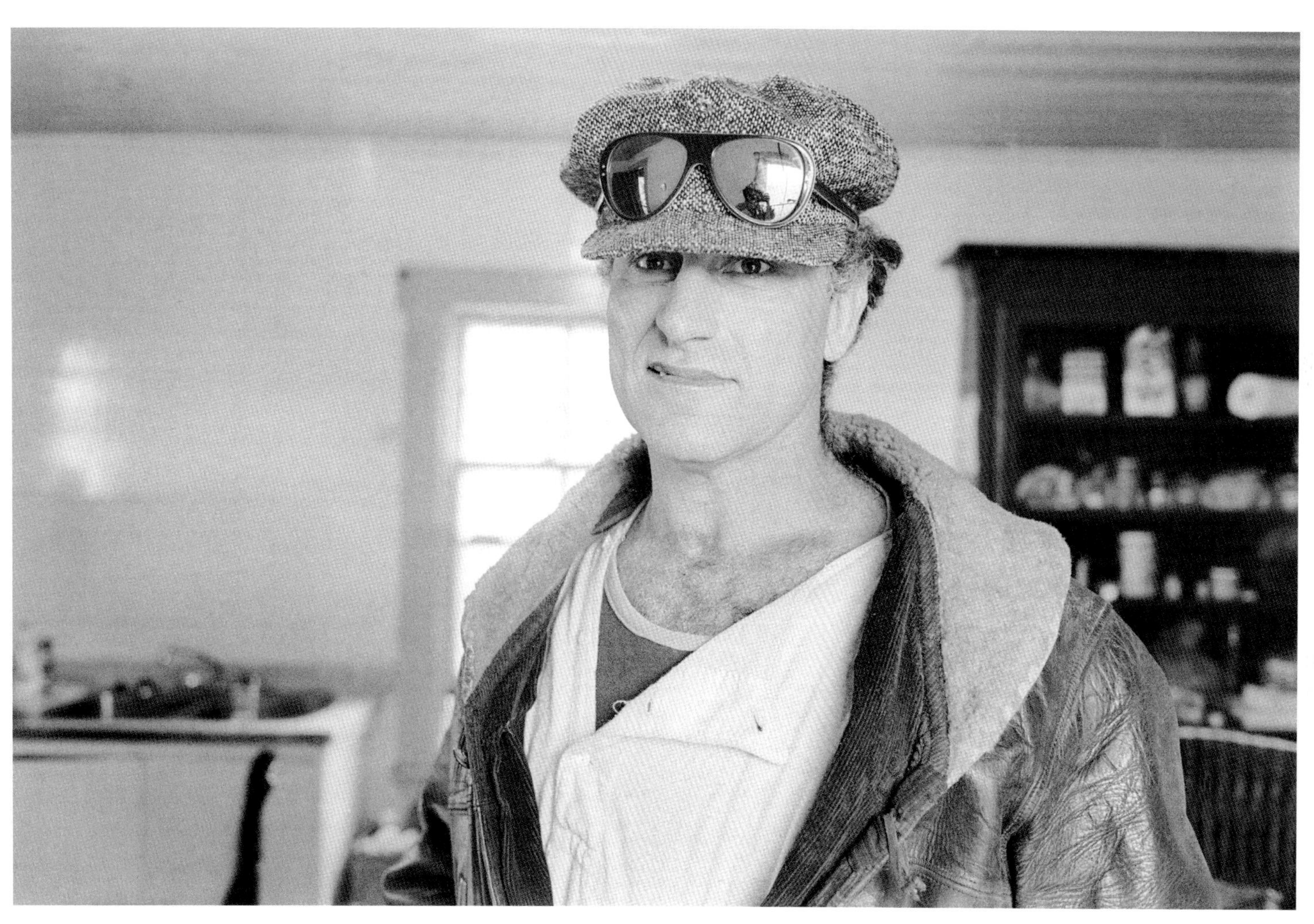

Costume drama #1: Richard

Summer on Cape Breton …
sunny days, happiness with friends,
many mosquitoes and black flies, daisies in the path.
A glorious walk to a waterfall to take a shower,
and outdoor plumbing behind every rock.
A little wooded area and a trail down to a beach.
I remember fishing one day with Phil …
Another time a party with lots of delicious food by JoAnne.
A 4th of July bonfire on the beach,
fire getting bigger and brighter as darkness fell.
Playing poker with Roberta and Rudy in their cabin.
All of us going to the horse races …
was it horse and buggy races or did I imagine the buggies …?
Helen had an efficient little cabin
just big enough for one person to stand in,
or maybe two slender people.
She had a marvelous white dog whose name escapes me …
sometimes that dog would sit in the sunshine
on the white cement step outside of Richard's house.

Pat Steir

Costume drama #3: Richard, Pat Steir,
Rudy, Tony Shafrazi, Lizzie Borden

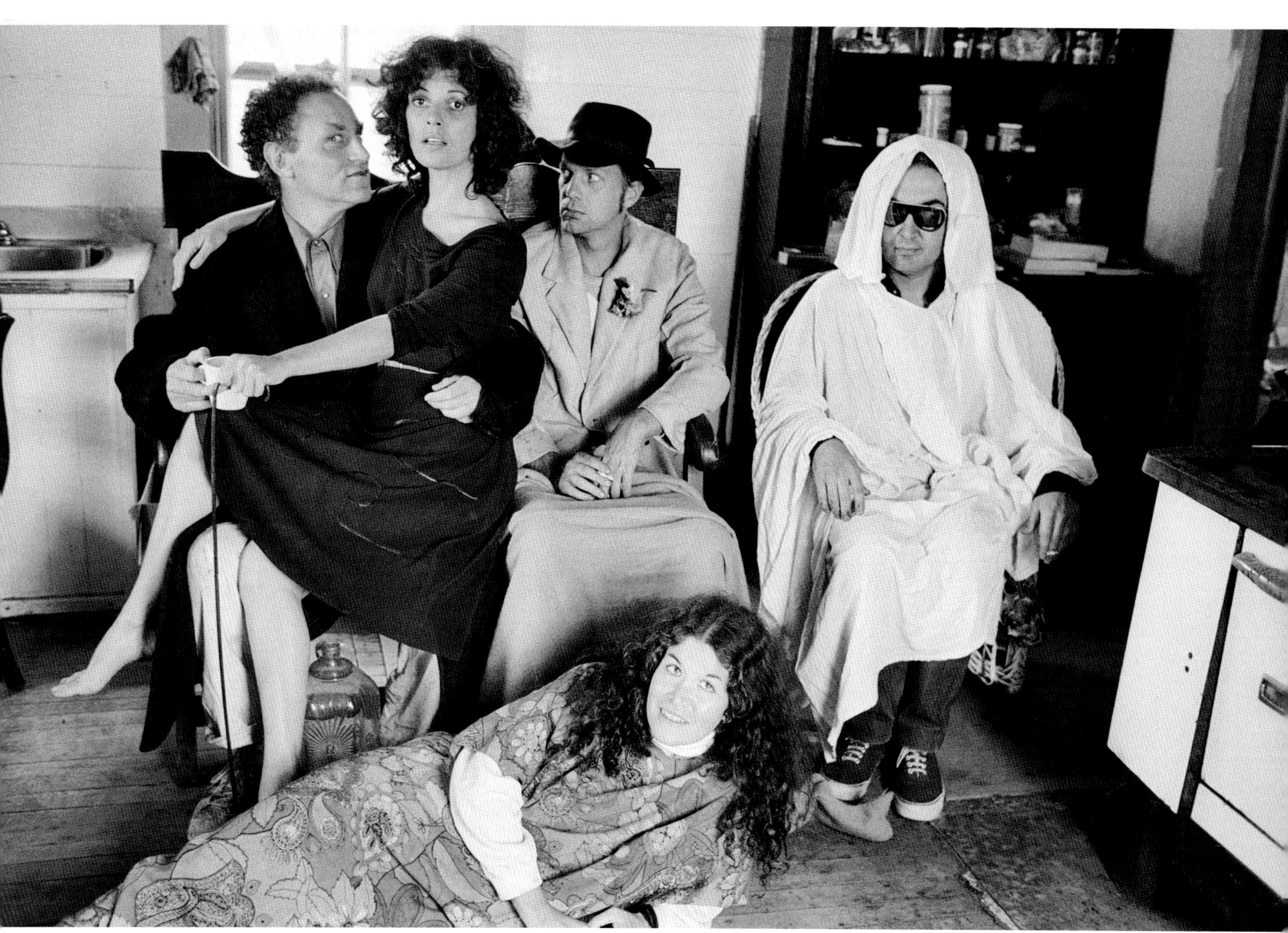

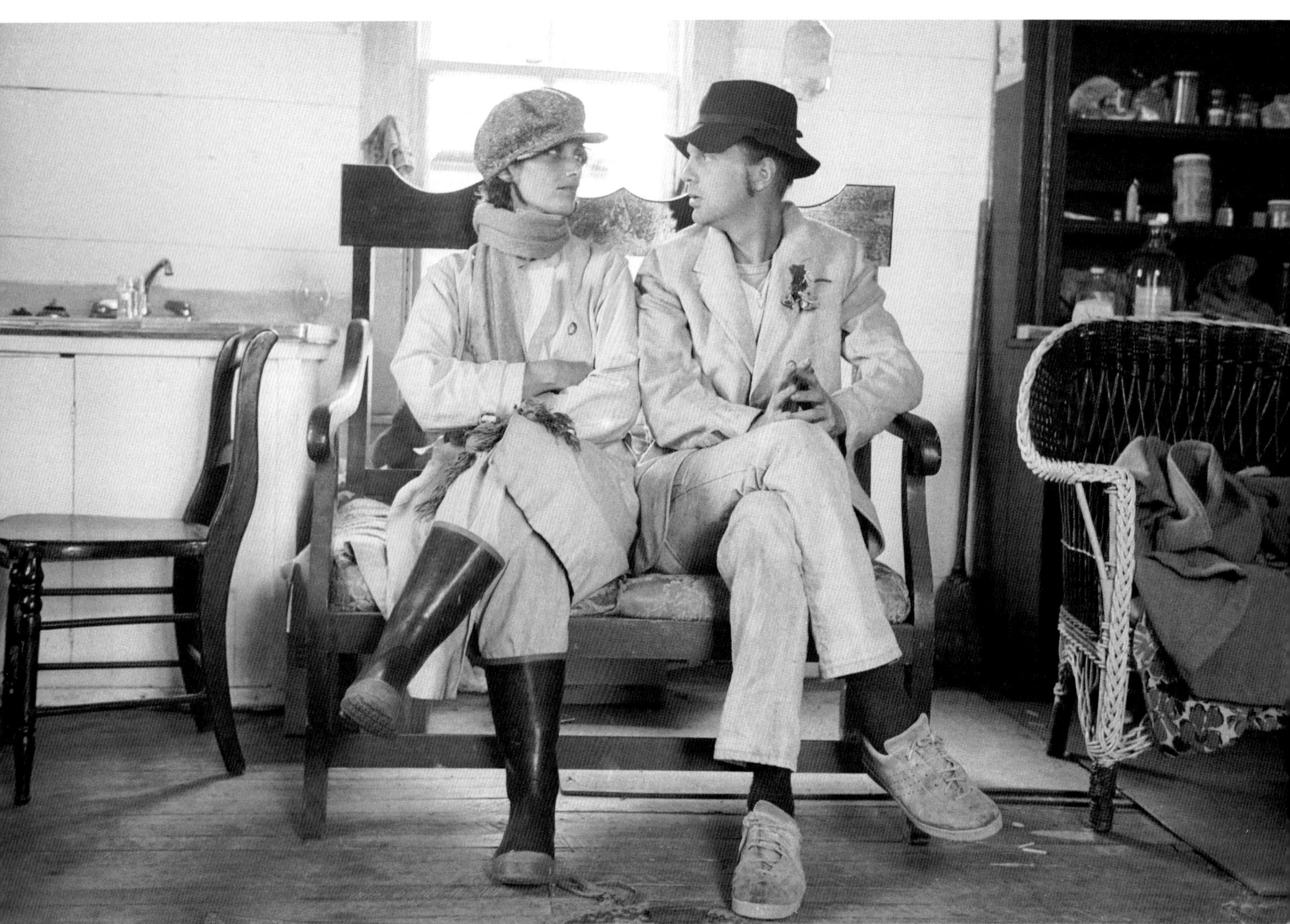

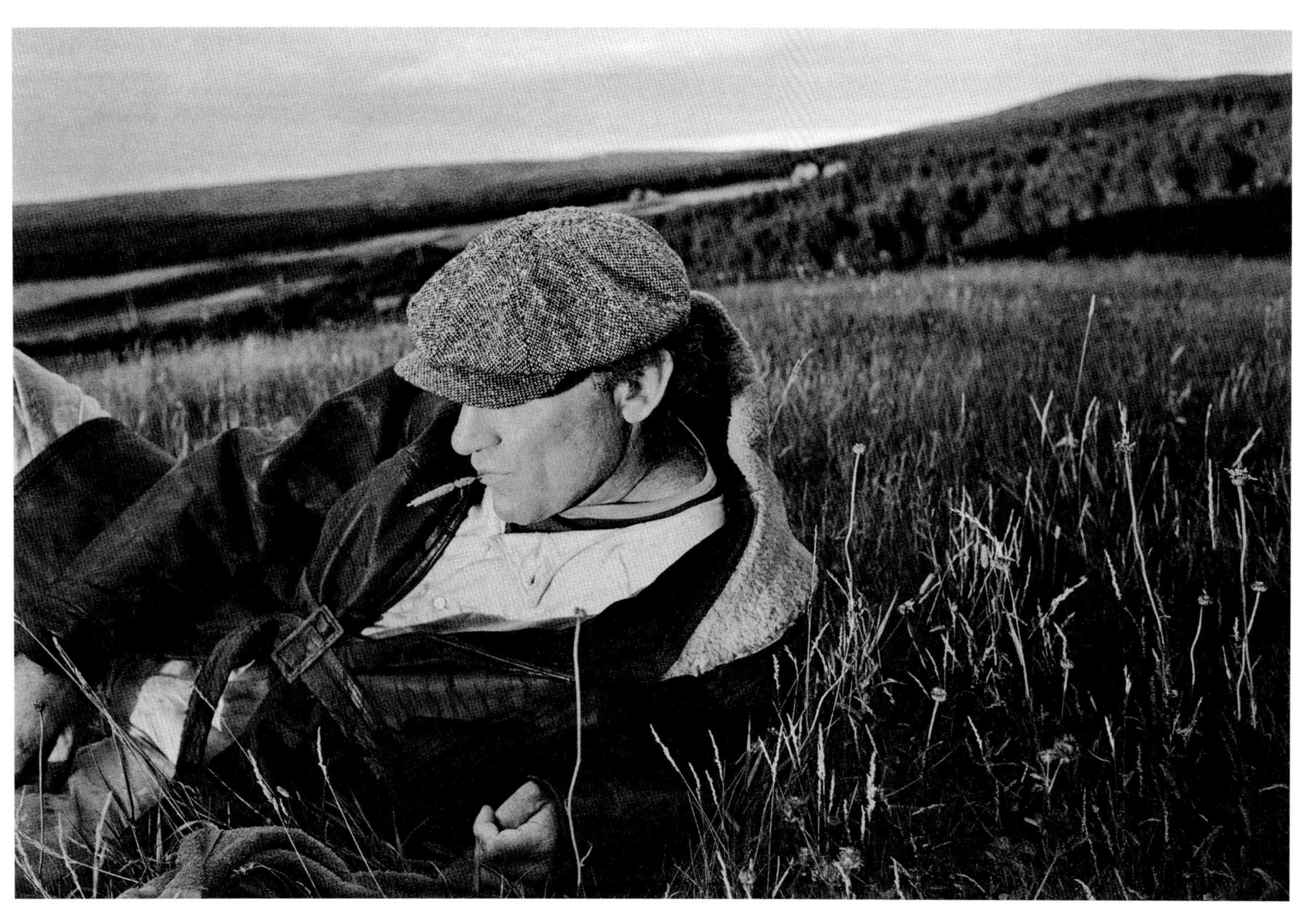

above, Richard at the golden hour

left, Costume drama #2: Roberta and Rudy

Jingle and I returned from an adventure covered in grime, ready for the shower. JoAnne rushed out to greet us. "Your children drowned," she said. She was frequently melodramatic. "Well, they didn't really drown because Joan and Rudy and Richard saved them. They almost drowned themselves too." Avrum, Nikolai, and Rafael had drifted out on a log, with Roberta's son, Greg. The wind picked up. The current between the beach and Sea-Wolf Island was tricky, and the kids got scared. Greg, who was a little older, swam back to shore, and alerted the adults. Our sons, Avrum and Nikolai said they could have swum back, but they didn't want to leave Rafael alone. He was the youngest, and didn't think he could make it. Rudy, Richard and Joan tried to launch the small boat, but couldn't. They stripped and put on the fins that were in the boat, and swam out. Joan grabbed Rafael. Even today, when they talk about the near catastrophe, my sons express envy of Rafael, who was rescued by bare naked Joan. Rudy almost went down himself, as he rescued one of the boys. Richard grabbed the other kid, and pulled him in. These were amazing friends, courageous and selfless, who risked their lives.

Steve Katz

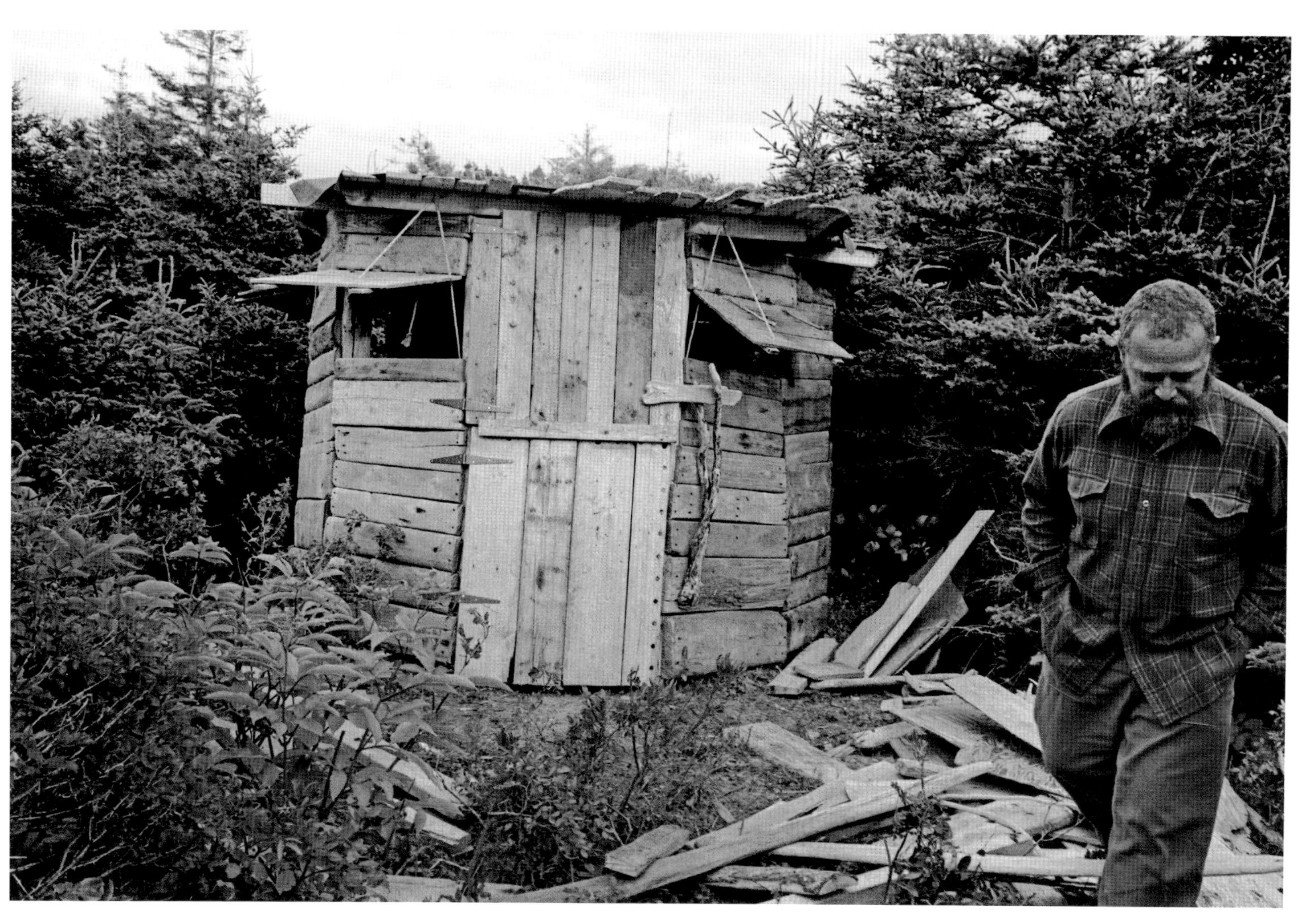

Steve Katz at his office

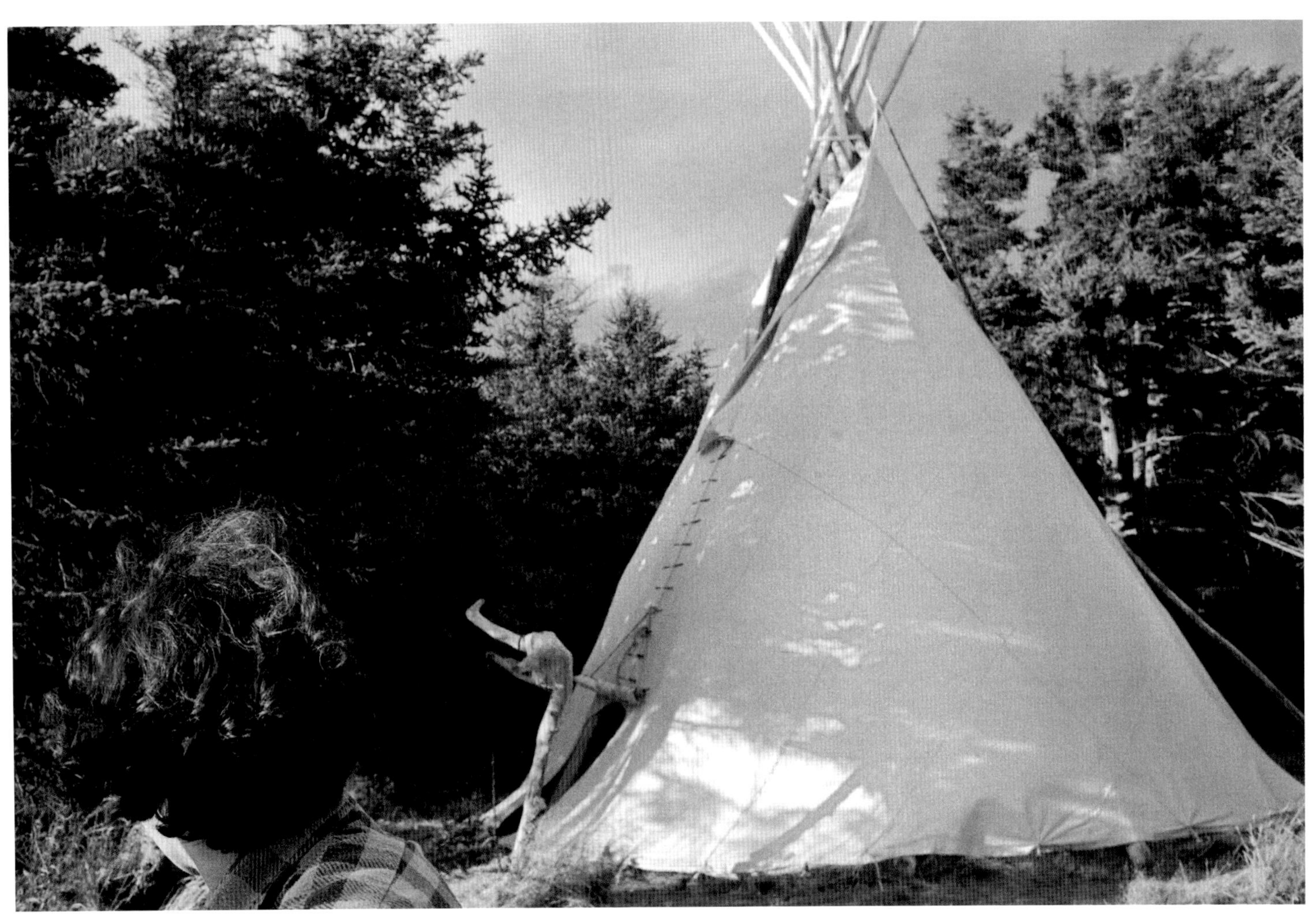

Steve's slightly imperfect teepee

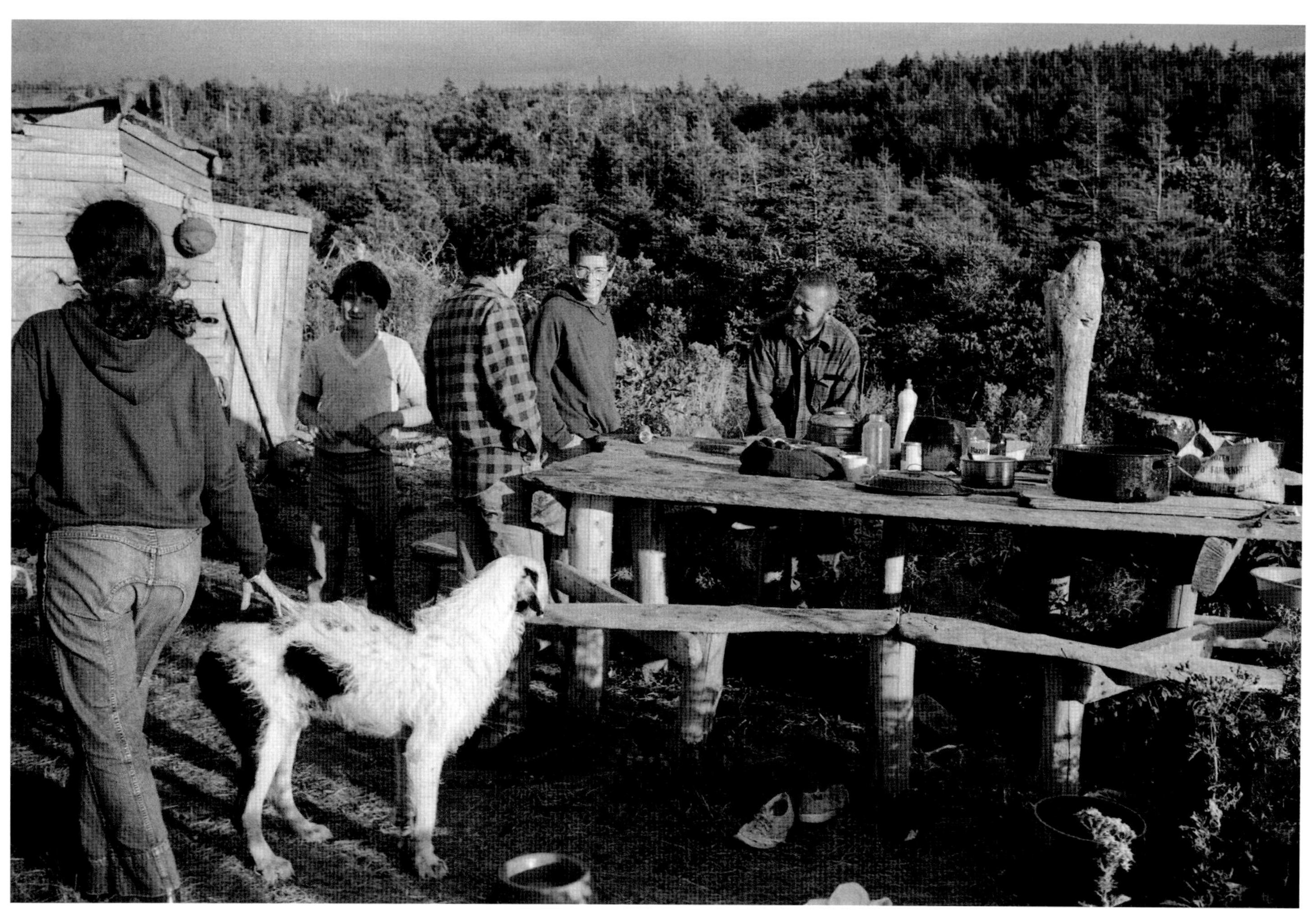

Katz's deli

One day, Roberta and I walk up a dirt road to Robert Frank's house in Mabou Mines. It's my first time there. Robert is a heavy dude. There is a presence he maintains that is quite intimidating. I ask Roberta how she is able to remain so casual and easy with him. She laughs, saying, "He's really like my old Jewish uncle." After that, I'm completely at ease.

DeeDee Halleck

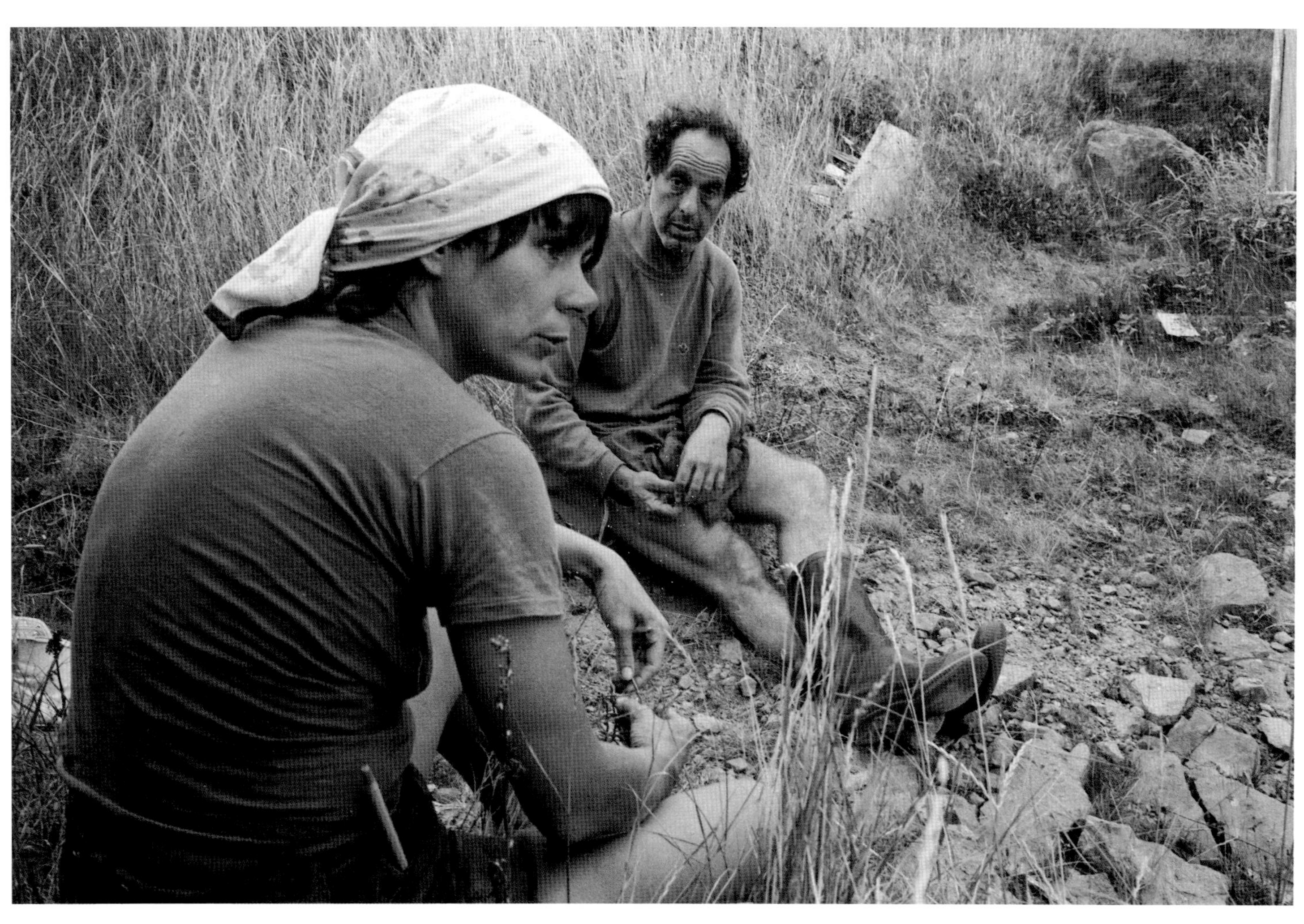

DeeDee and Robert tuning up for the shoot

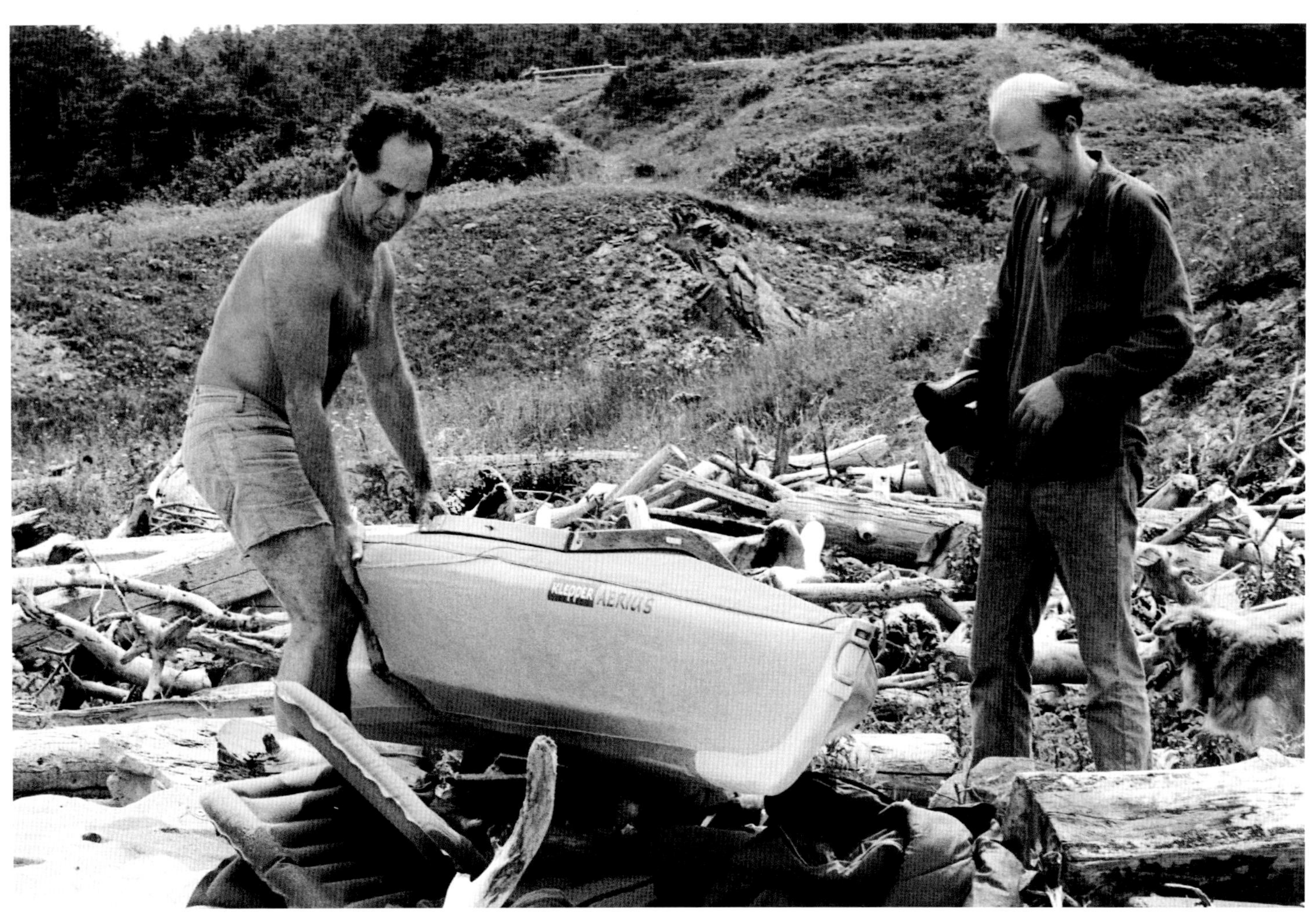

above, Robert and Rudy go boating

right, Rudy and Robert in the kayak, June looks on

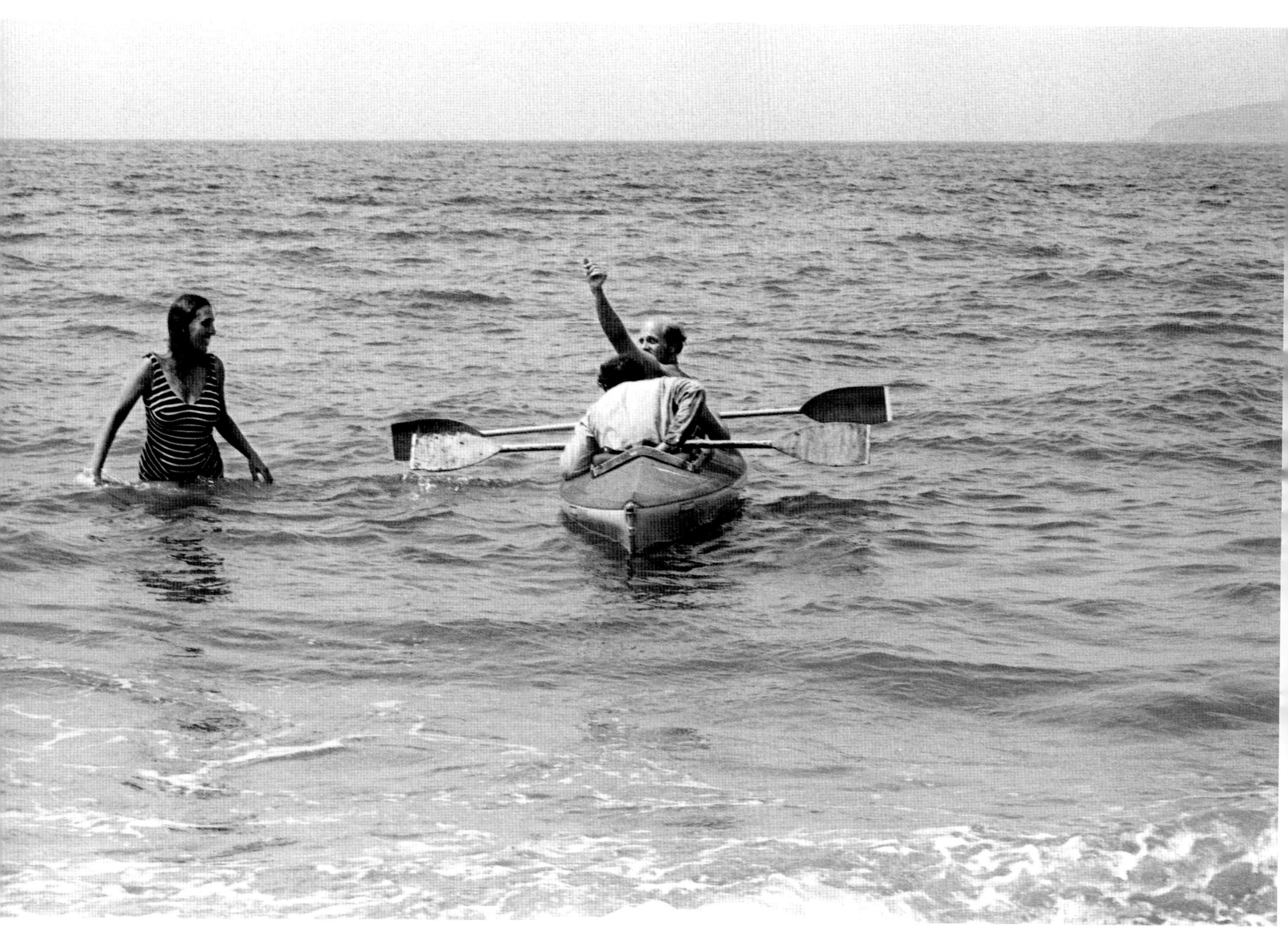

In 1975, Rudy and Robert Frank decided Margaree Island would be a perfect location to shoot a small, absurdist film they called, *Keep Busy*. Rudy wrote the script and directed the language, Robert directed the action. Together they urged the players to improvise outrageously. JoAnne Akalaitis and other actors from the Mabou Mines Theater Company ran through the barren landscape shouting unintelligibly. Joan Jonas explored the shacks, swinging on the rafters, howling like a she-wolf, Richard Serra kicking planks out of a cabin wall, June Leaf chanting homemade mantras, Richard on water, Joan on fire. David Warrilow, an eccentric lighthouse keeper in silken neckerchief and Crombie coat, declaimed Becketty riffs from his broken window, giving the populace their daily news by means of a transistor radio broadcasting Atlantic weather conditions. The movie was a great collaborative effort that involved the whole community and captures a sidelong glimpse of our group's eccentricity.

Roberta Neiman

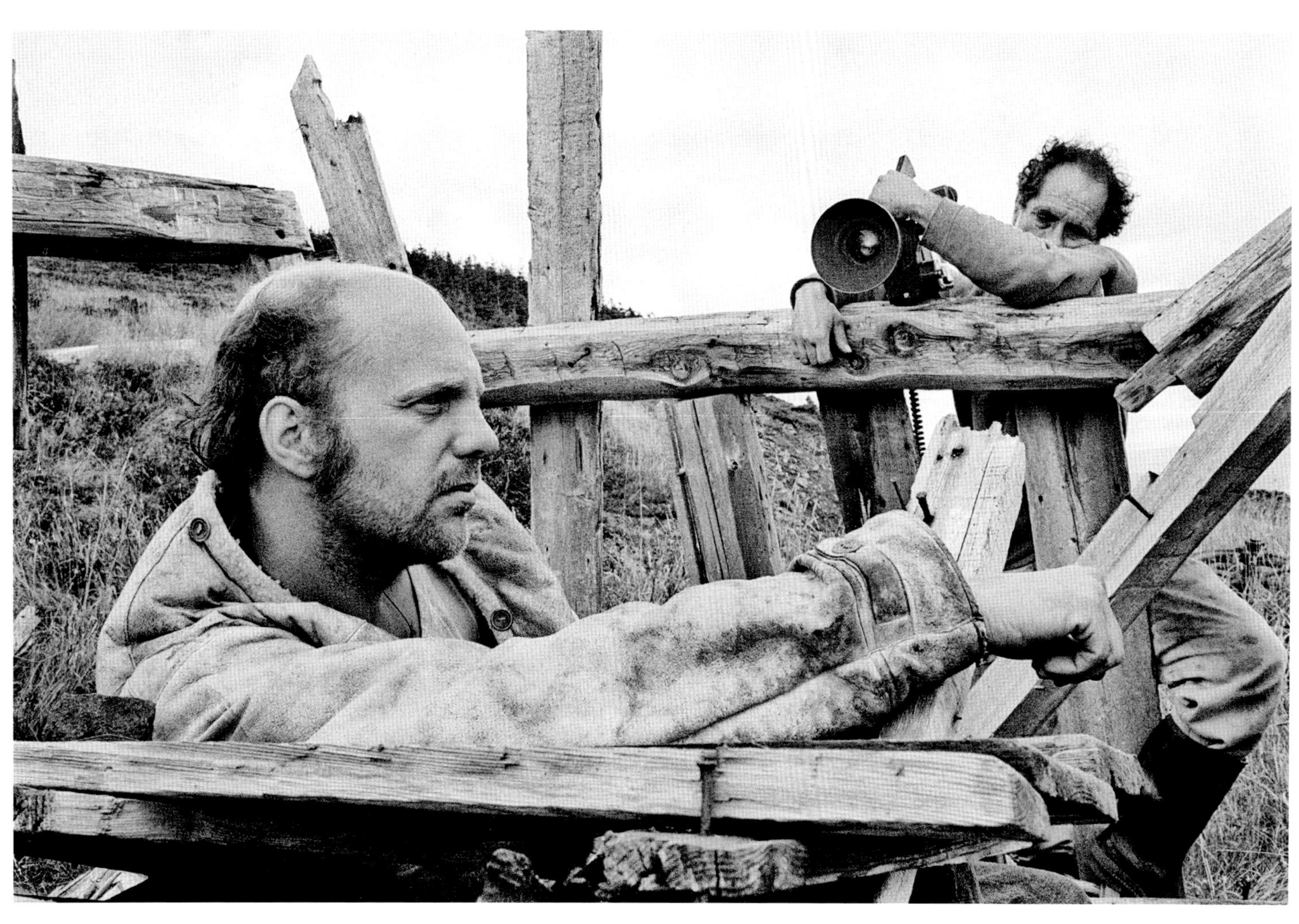

The brains behind *Keep Busy*

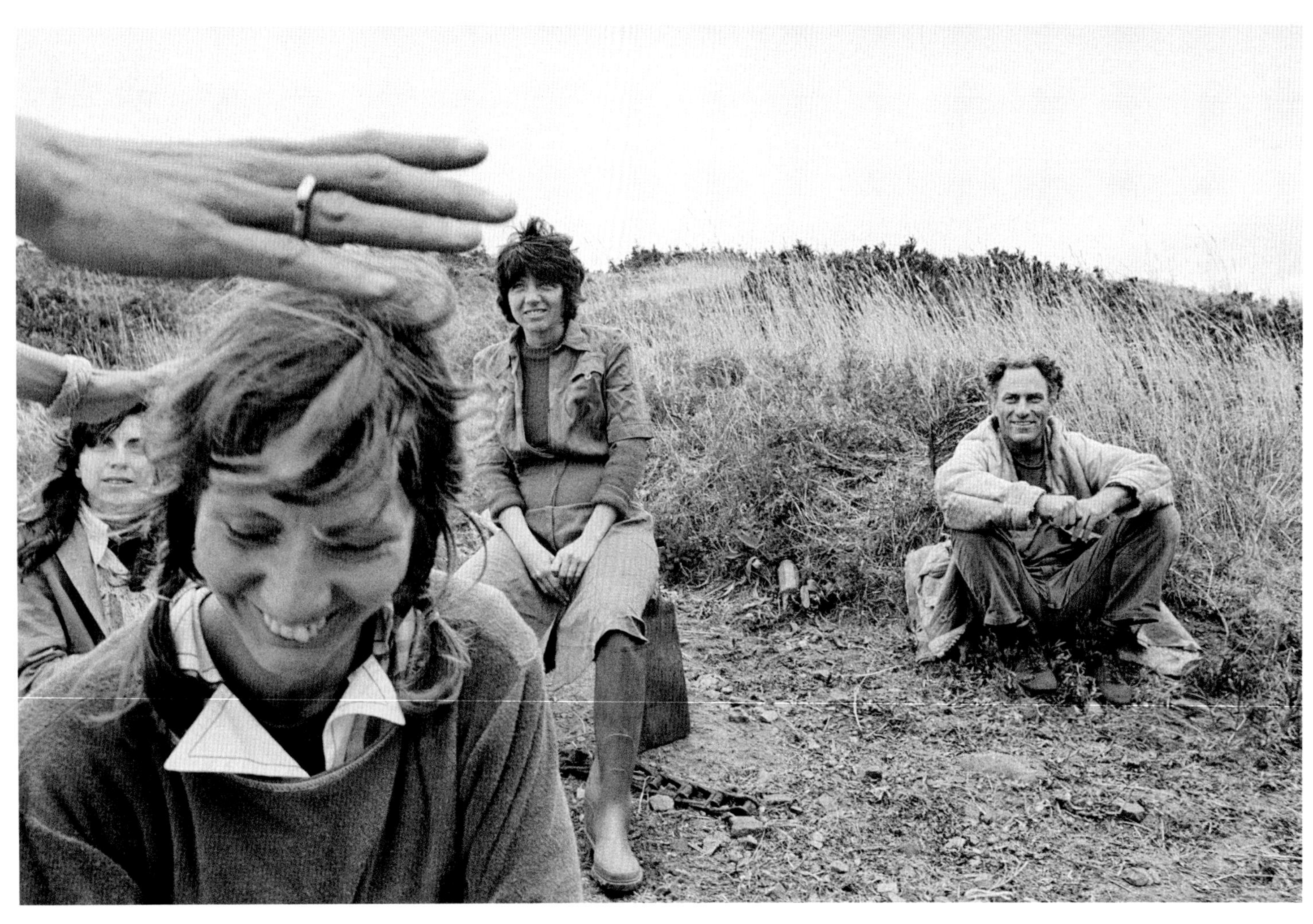

above, On location. The cast prepares

right, Joan warms up around the campfire

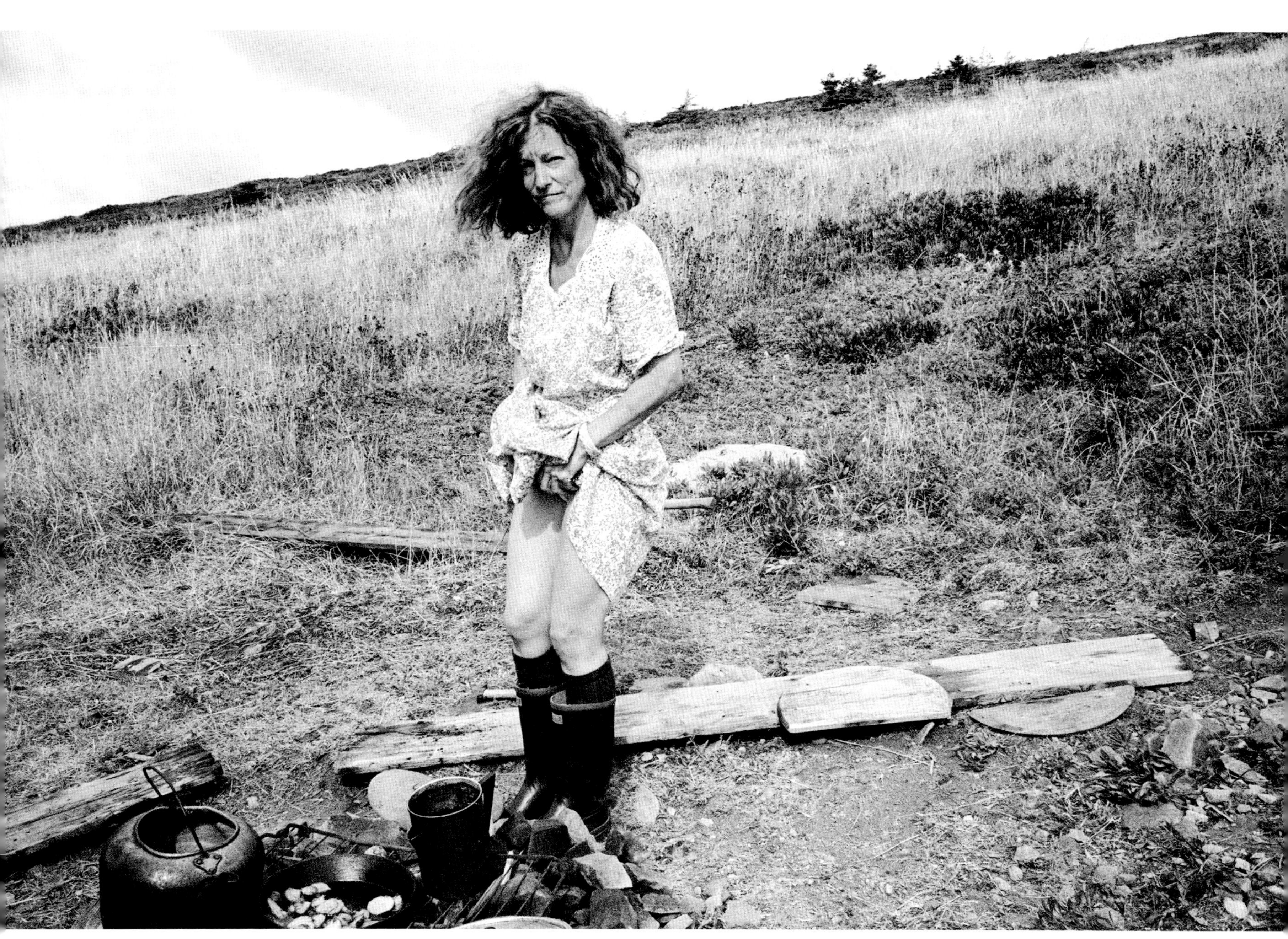

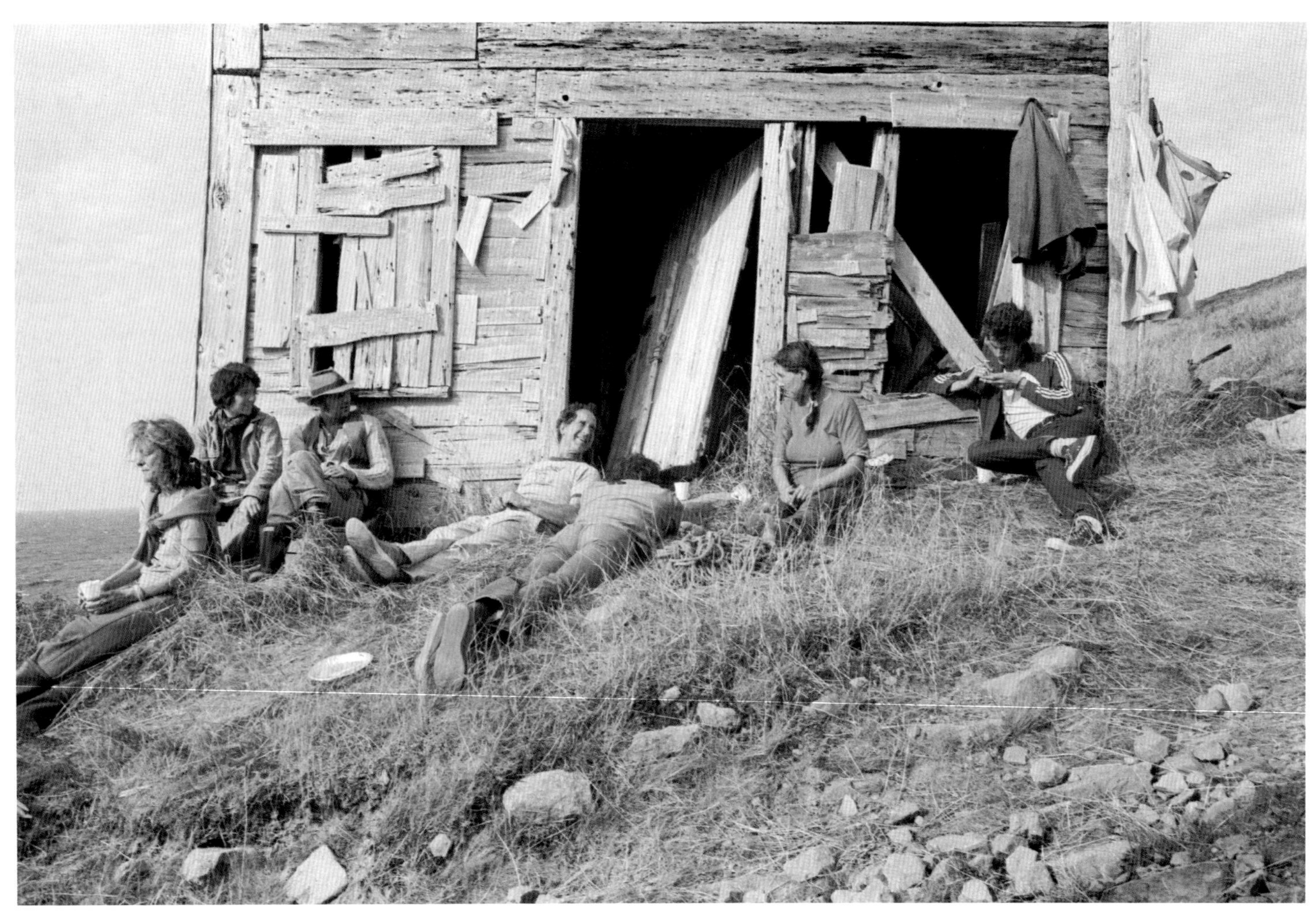

On set at Margaree

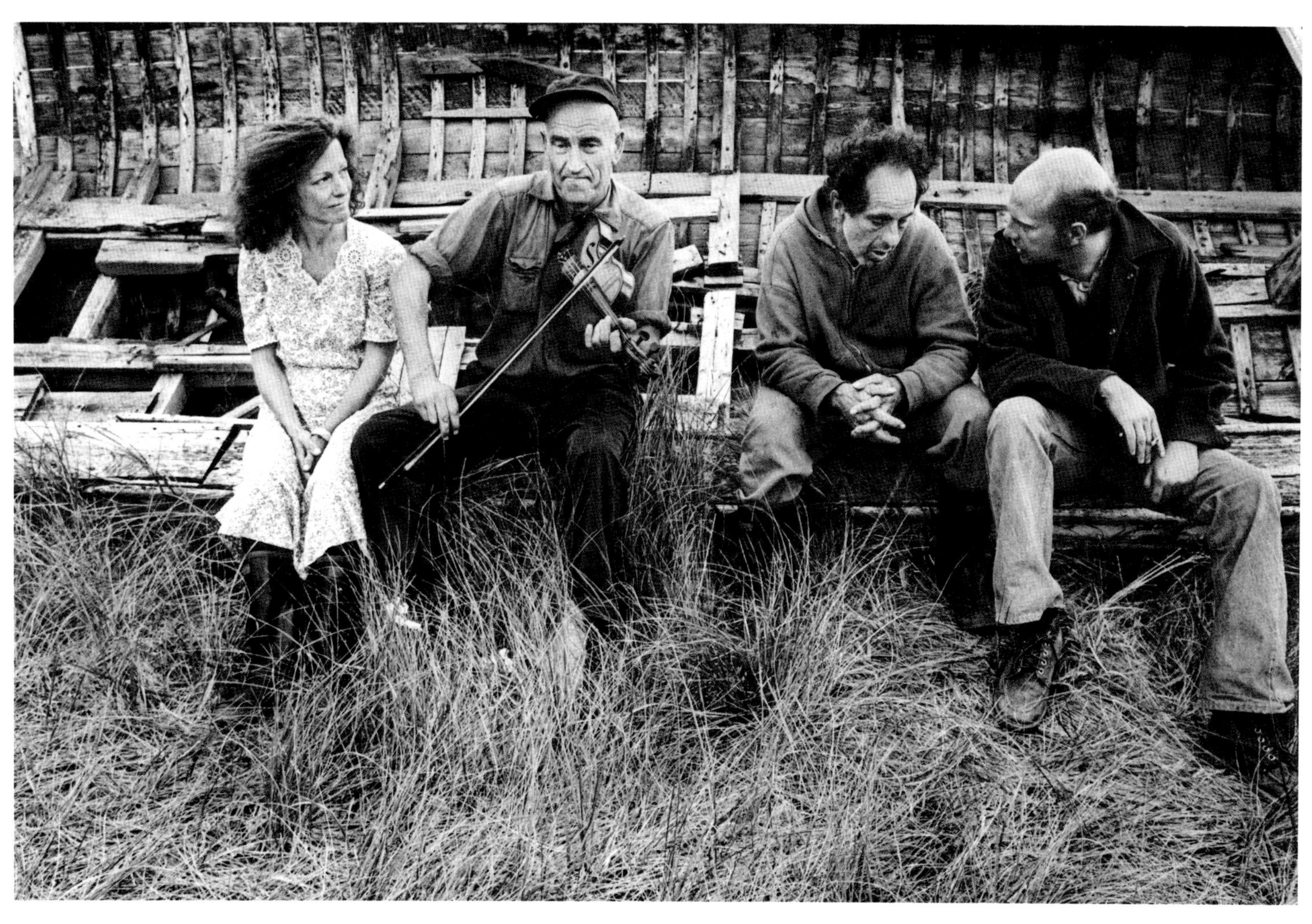

A Breton fiddler serenades
Joan, Robert, and Rudy

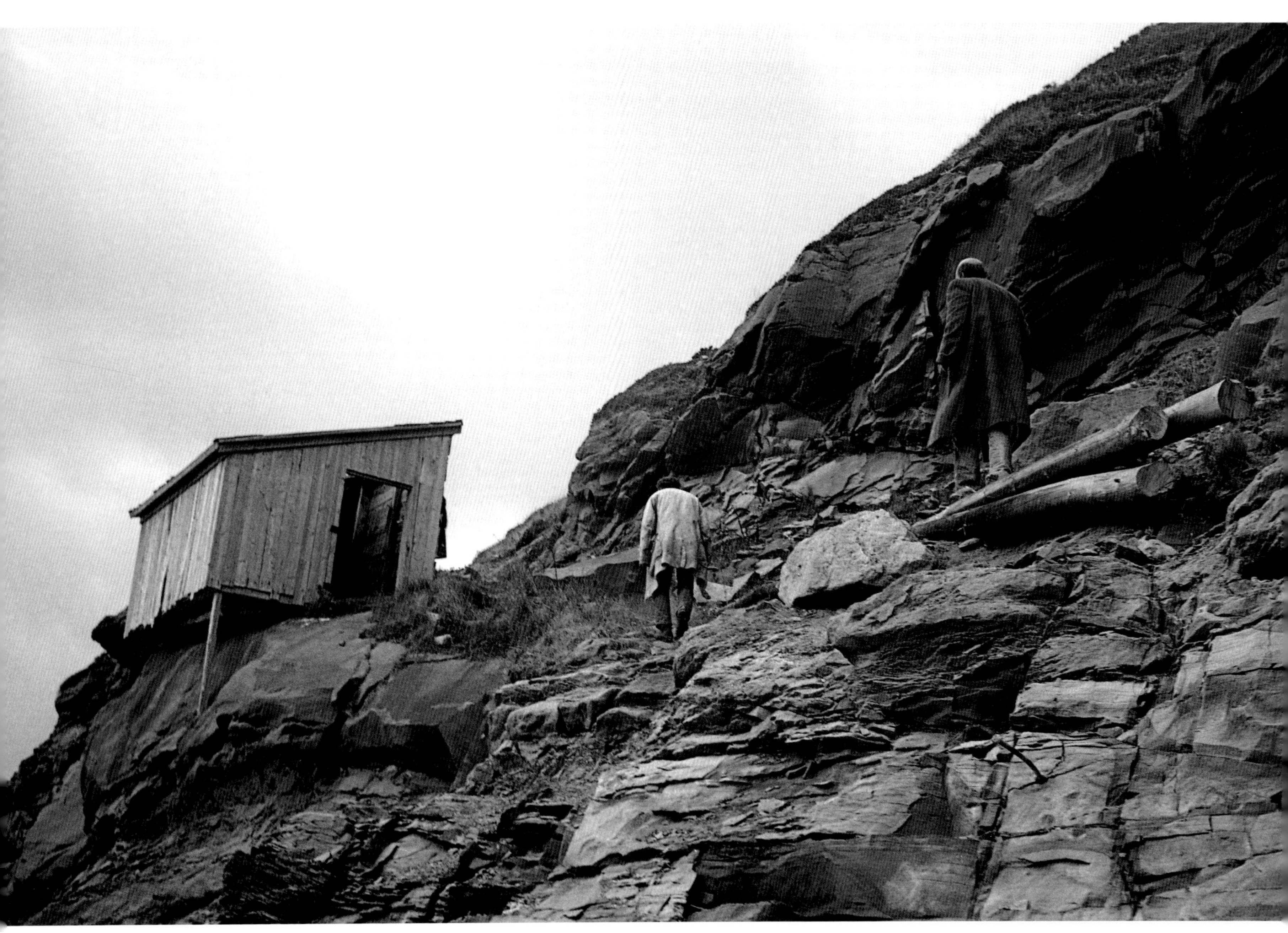

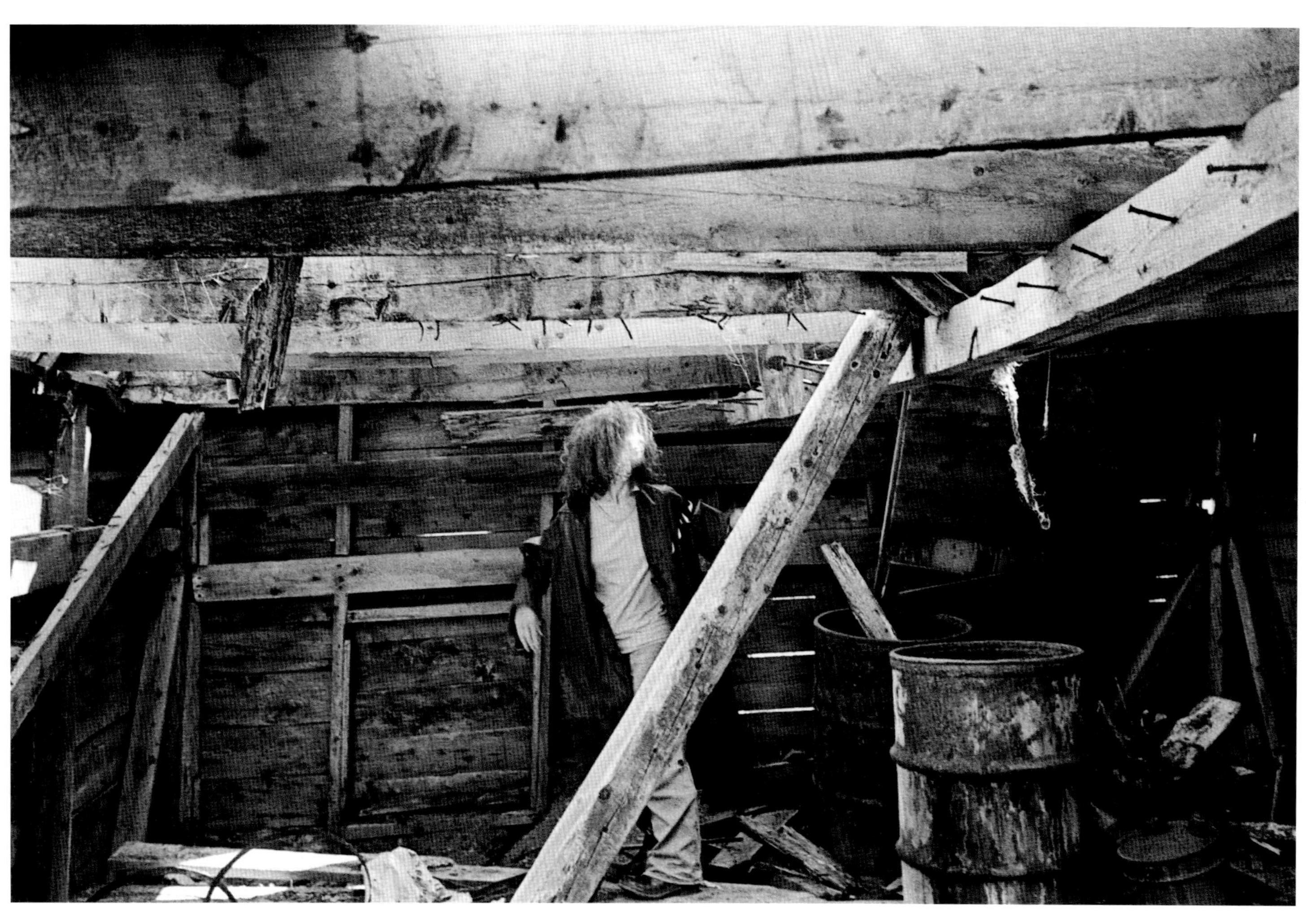

above, Joan channeling her spirit guide

left, Robert and Rudy scouting locations

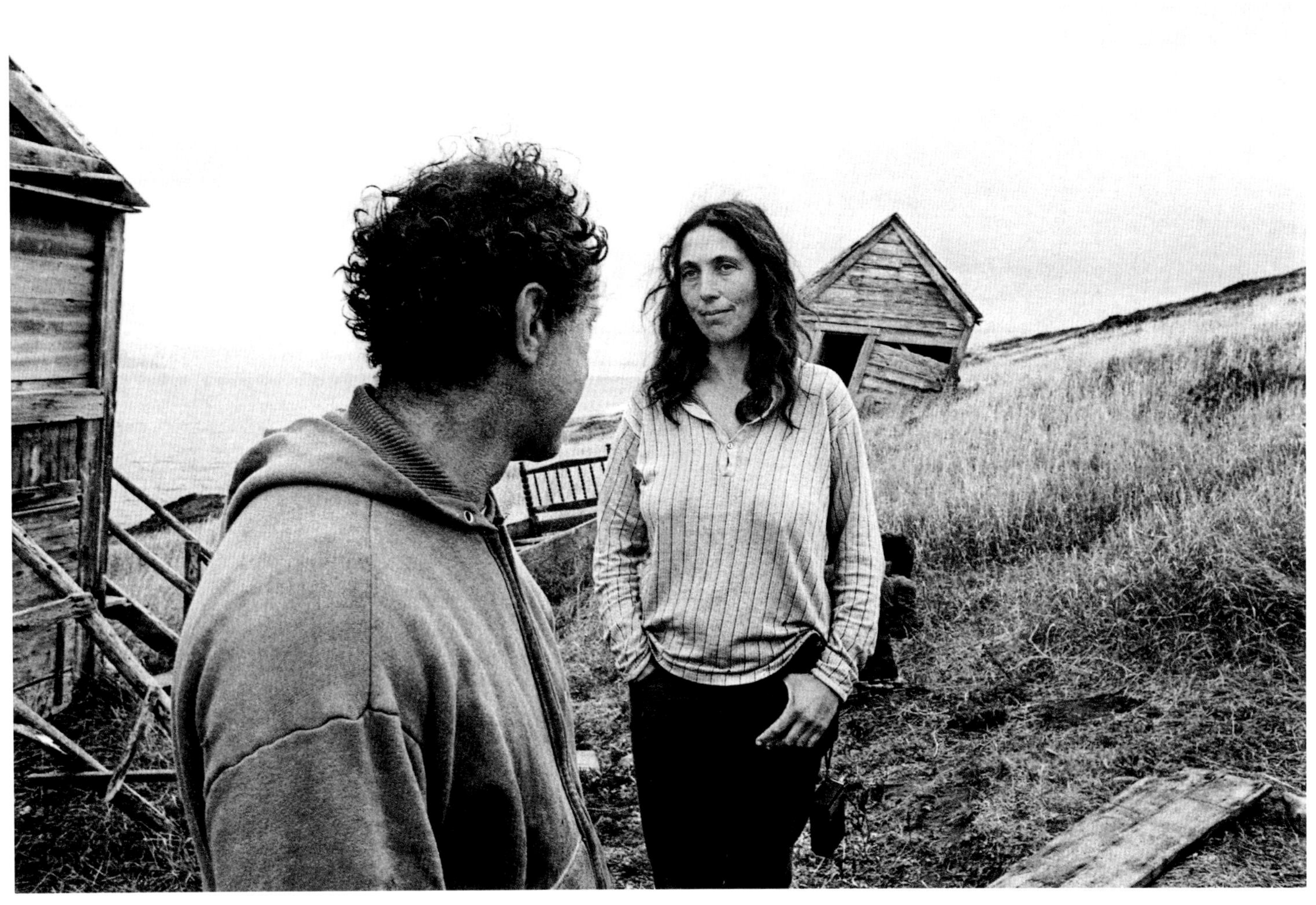

Robert confers with his muse, June

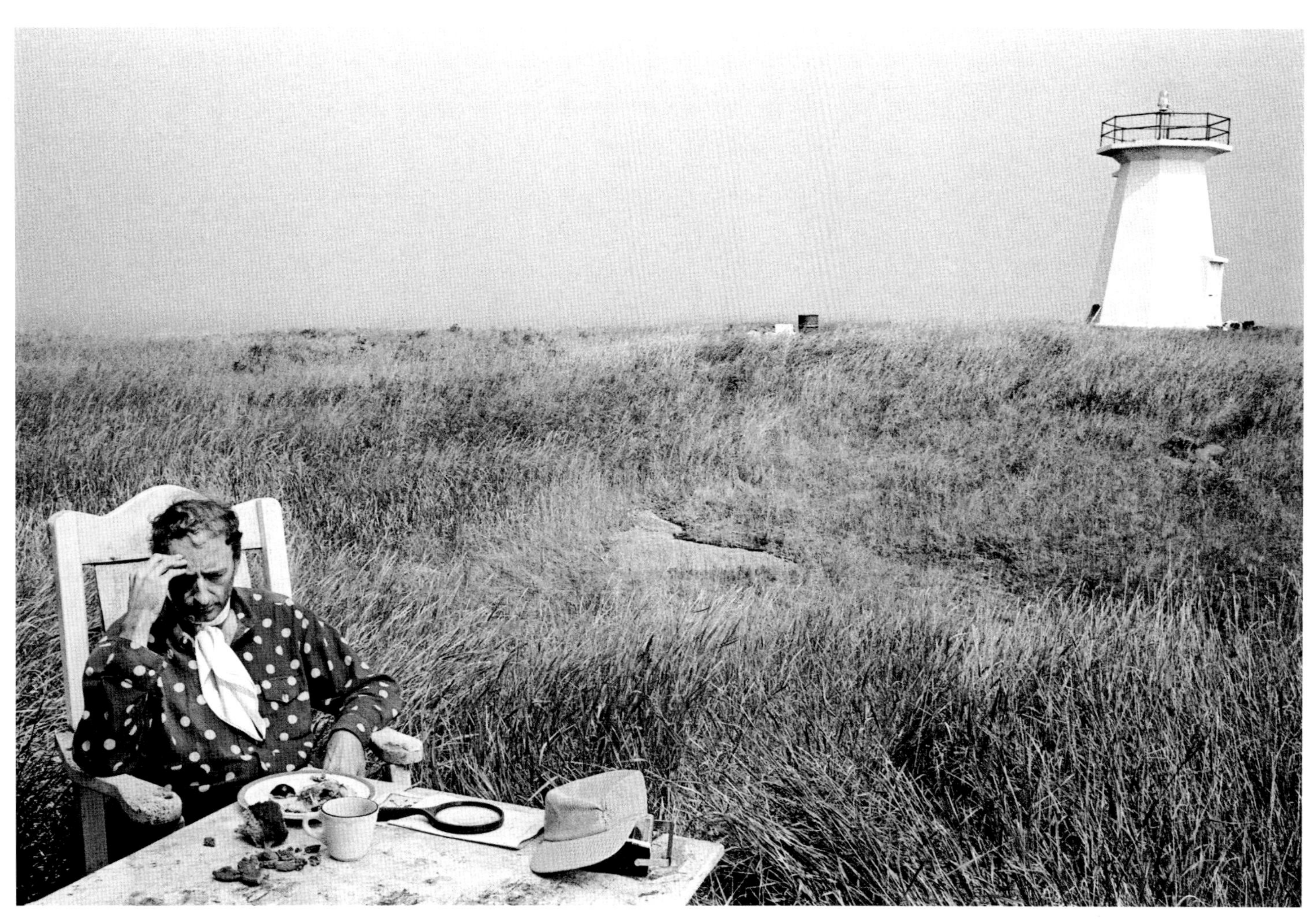

David Warrilow in character
as the Lighthouse Keeper

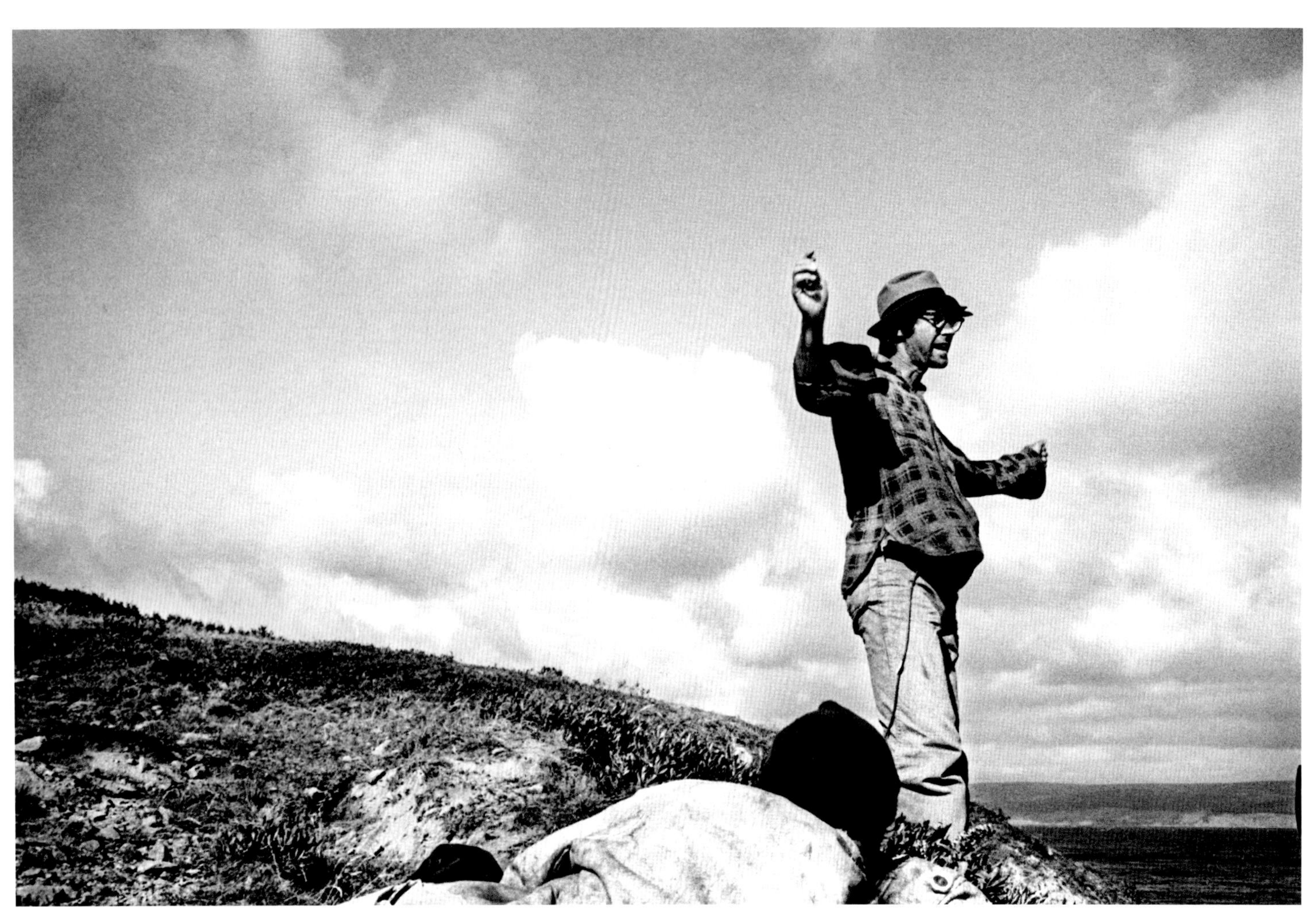

above, Bill Raymond declaims
to the blue skies

right, Joan at the edge of the world

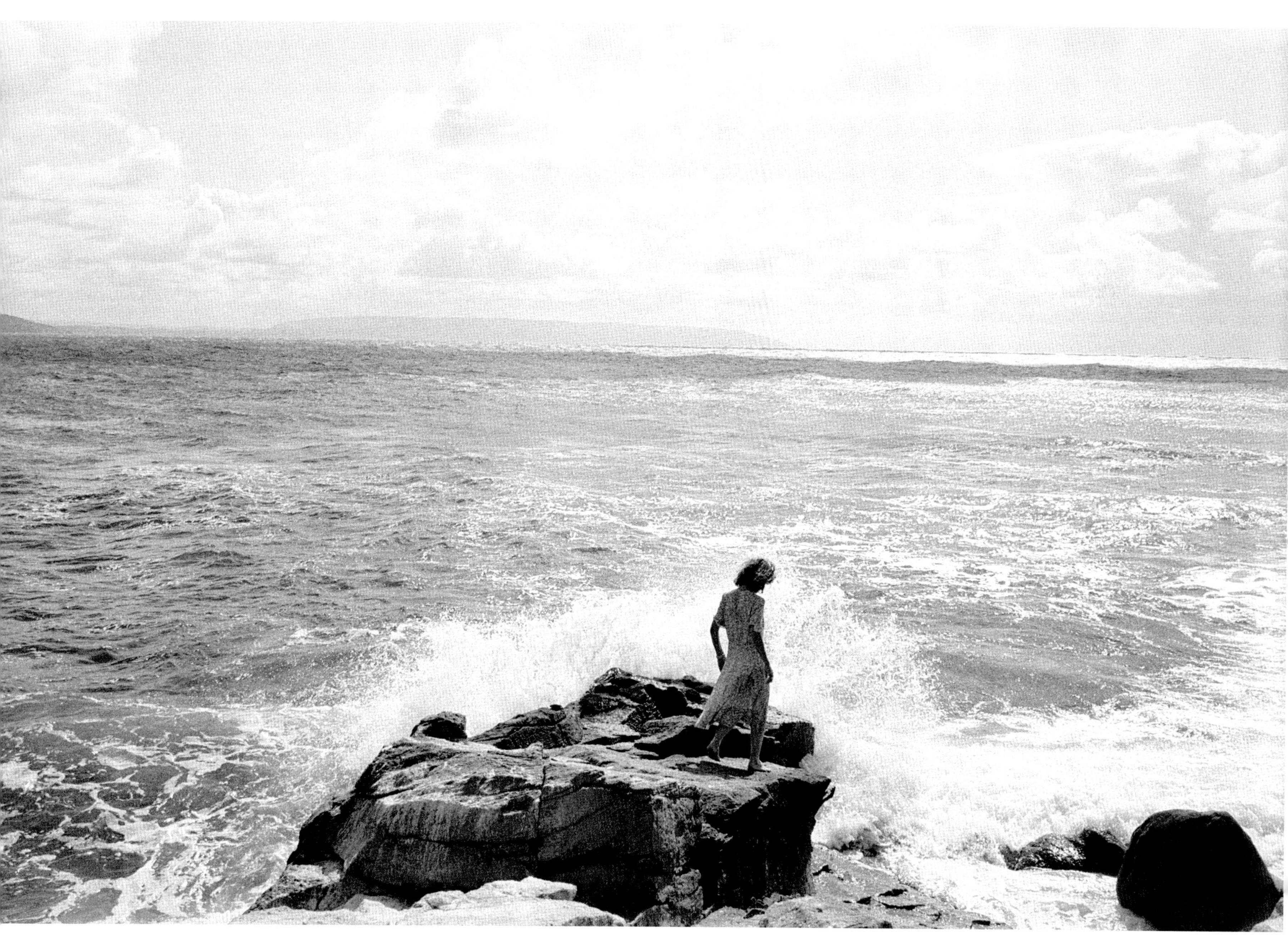

I watched the ocean all the time. Sometimes the water was quiet, abalone green, transparent as a pool, but often it swelled and its milky froth clamored against the wind. The island disappeared sometimes in the mists, or rose like the toque on the head of a jazz drummer (say Art Blakey) in the distant thunder.

Steve Katz

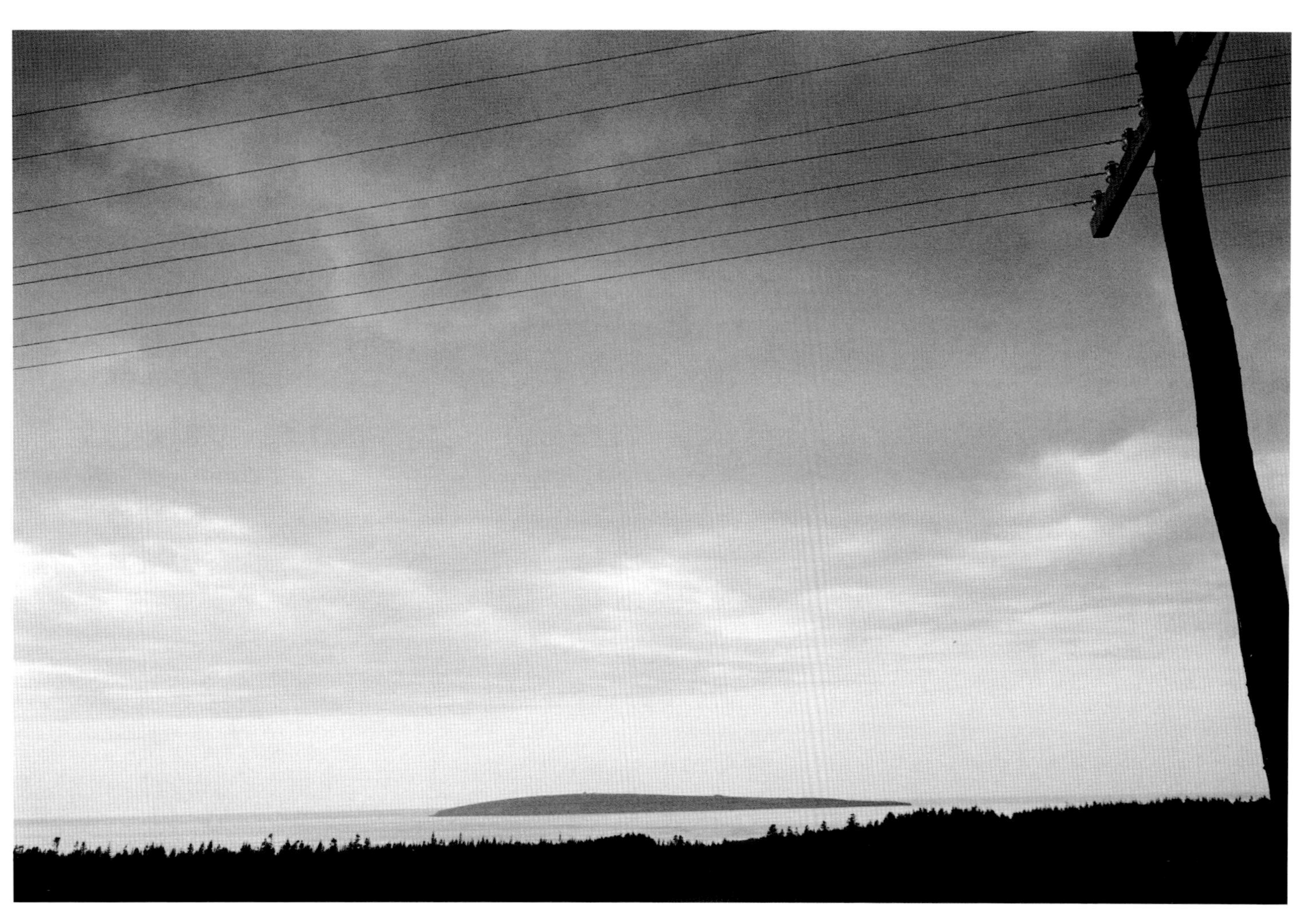

Margaree from the road

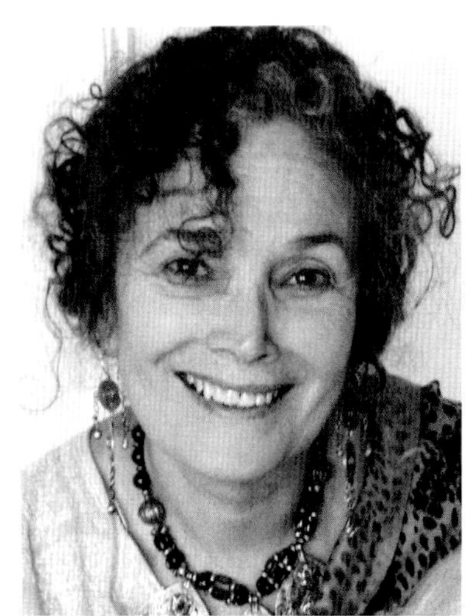

ROBERTA NEIMAN

Photographer

After living and working in NYC as a photographer and videographer for several artists including Joan Jonas, Richard Serra and others, Neiman returned to L.A. in 1980. She remained there for the next fifteen years, working as an interior architect and designer. In 2005, she resumed her photographic career, and established a new home and studio in Oaxaca, Mexico, where she still lives. Neiman shot the photographs in this book over a five-year period, 1970-75, while summering with this eclectic group of artists gathered on the far Atlantic coast. The original prints were developed in Cape Breton's saltwater, and many were lost over time. These images are what remain of an idyllic period of blissful isolation.

JOANNE AKALAITIS

b. 1937, Chicago, IL

Avant-garde Lithuanian-American theatre director and writer. Founding director of Mabou Mines Company. Akalaitis lives and works in New York City.

ROBERT FRANK

b. 1924, Zürich, Switzerland.

Swiss-American photographer and filmmaker. His first book, *The Americans* (1958), is considered a major influence on 20th Century photography. He shares his life and work with June Leaf, in New York City and Nova Scotia.

PHILIP GLASS

b. 1937, Baltimore, MD.

Widely regarded as the one of the most influential avant-garde composers and musicians of the 20th century. Worked on and refined many of his operas and other major compositions under the blissful stimulation of Cape Breton.

DEEDEE HALLECK

b. 1940, St. Louis, MO.

Media activist, video and film maker, co-founder of the Deep Dish Satellite Network, the first grassroots community television network.

JOAN JONAS

b. 1936, New York, NY.

Visual artist and pioneer of video and performance art. Regarded as one of the most important artists to emerge from the burgeoning New York scene of the early 1970s. Jonas maintains her practice in a house and studio on Cape Breton and a loft in New York City.

STEVE KATZ

b. 1935, New York, NY.

Fiction writer. Author of over thirty books and other publications. In 1978 he became the director of the creative writing program at the University of Colorado at Boulder. Katz has also worked as a miner, a dairy farmer, and a teacher of Tai Chi Chuan.

NIKOLAI KATZ

b. 1959, New York, NY.

Son of Steve. Architect, founded his company, Nikolai Katz Architect, in 1998, in New York City.

RICHARD (DICKIE) LANDRY

b. 1938, Cecilia, LA.

Photographer, musician, composer, artist. He was a founding member of the original Philip Glass Ensemble in 1969.

JUNE LEAF

b. 1929, Chicago, IL.

Abstract artist and kinetic sculptor. With her husband Robert Frank, she continues to divide her time between New York City and Nova Scotia.

MABOU MINES

Avant-garde Theater Company.

Mabou Mines is a collective of artists, ideas and approaches established in Cape Breton in 1970 by David Warrilow, Lee Breuer, Ruth Maleczech, JoAnne Akalaitis and Philip Glass.

GREG NEIMAN

b. 1958, Los Angeles, CA.

"Greg first came to Cape Breton when he was 11 years old. He had an enthusiastic eye and sensibility about the place, and learned a great deal from the determination of the artists around him." R.N.

PHILIP GLASS ENSEMBLE

Musical group founded by composer Philip Glass in 1968 to serve as a performance outlet for his experimental minimalist music. The Philip Glass Ensemble continues to perform and record today, under the musical direction of keyboardist and conductor Michael Riesman.

RICHARD SERRA

b. 1938, San Francisco, CA.

Serra is a world-renowned American artist best known for his large-scale steel works. He lives and works in New York City and on Cape Breton, Nova Scotia.

KEITH SONNIER

b. 1941, Mamou, LA.

Sonnier was one of the first artists to use light in sculpture in the late 1960s, and currently works with a wide variety of other materials, including neon and fluorescent lights, aluminum, copper, wood and glass. He lives and works in New York City and Sagaponack, Long Island.

PAT STEIR

b. 1940, Newark, NJ.

Widely regarded as one of the finest living American abstract painters. For the past forty years, she has lived and worked primarily in New York City.

JIM STRAHS

1943-2011.

Writer and director. A playwright and novelist based in New York City. His work was frequently performed by Mabou Mines and later by the Wooster Group in New York, among others. He died in Vermont in 2011.

HELEN TWORKOV

b. 1943, New York, NY.

Editor and writer. Founding editor of Tricycle, (1990), a controversial Buddhist Review, the first of its kind. Since 2006 she has been a student of the Kagyu and Nyingma Tibetan master Yongey Mingyur Rinpoche.

RUDY WURLITZER

b. 1937, Cincinnati, OH.

American novelist and screenwriter. Wurlitzer is one of the great but lesser known American writers to emerge intact from the epic craziness of the late 1960s. Novelist and screenwriter of such legendary works as *Two Lane Blacktop, Nog* and *Slow Fade.*

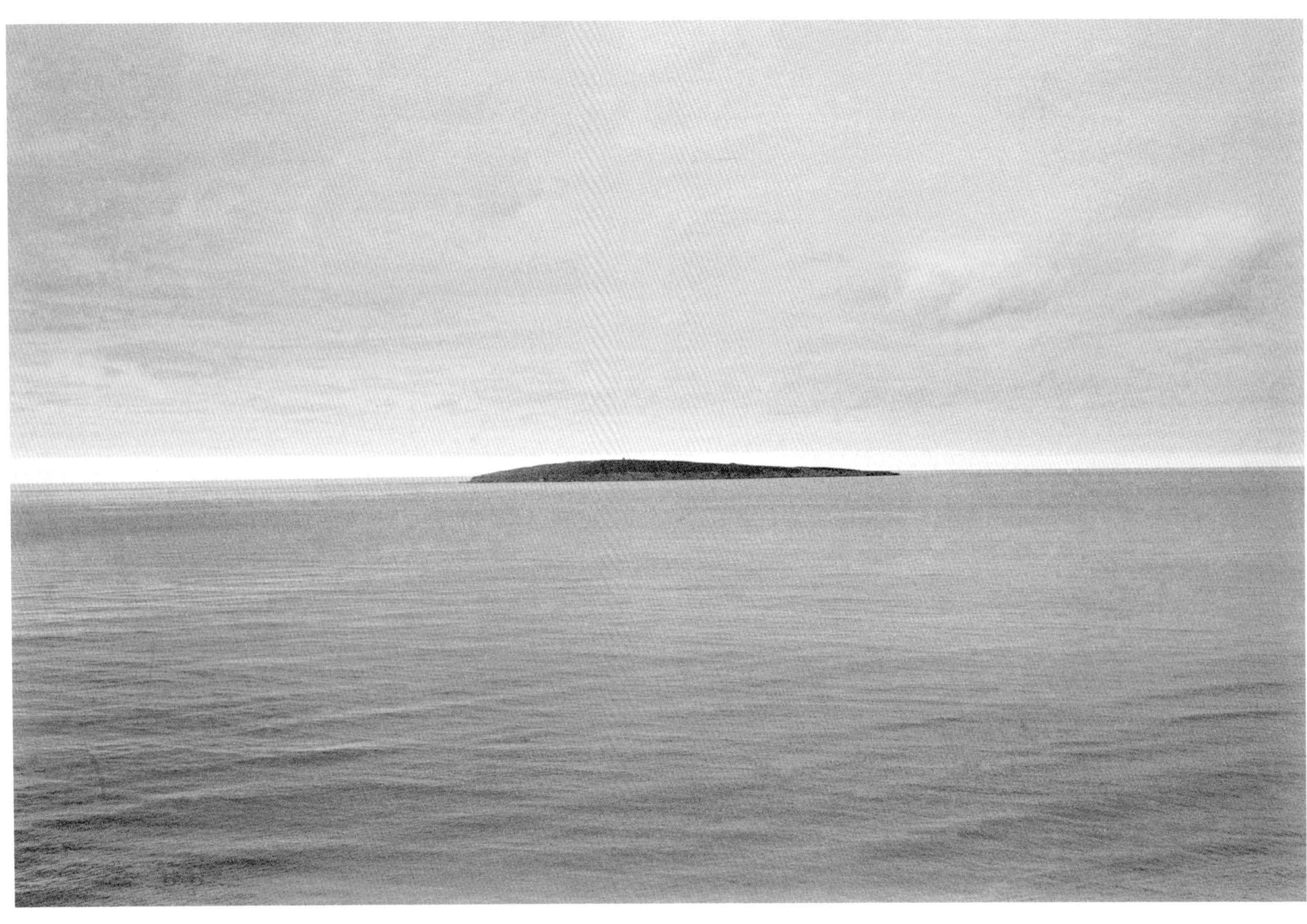